SELECTED WRITINGS

JAMES LEIGH HUNT was born in Middlesex in 1784 and educated at Christ's Hospital School. His first book of poems appeared when he was seventeen. In 1808 he and his brother founded a radical weekly paper, *The Examiner*. An allegedly libellous article published in the paper about the Prince Regent led to a heavy fine and two year's imprisonment for the brothers. Hunt's wife joined him in prison, from where he continued to edit the paper. Hunt's circle of friends included Byron, Hazlitt and Lamb and he promoted the work of Keats and Shelley in *The Examiner*. In 1821 he travelled to Italy to join Byron and Shelley in launching a new periodical, *The Liberal*. Only four issues were published and he returned to London in 1825. *Lord Byron and his Contemporaries* (1828), an unflattering appraisal that made him unpopular, was based on that experience. In addition to poetry and journalism, Hunt's works include volumes of literary criticism, plays, a devotional work, and his *Autobiography* (1850). He died in 1859.

DAVID JESSON-DIBLEY was the Head of English at Christ's Hospital School before his retirement. He subsequently became a freelance lecturer in English literature, chiefly for the Extra-Mural Department of London University. He is a longstanding member of the Friends of S.T. Coleridge.

Fyfield*Books* aim to make available some of the great classics of British and European literature in clear, affordable formats, and to restore often neglected writers to their place in literary tradition.

Fyfield*Books* take their name from the Fyfield elm in Matthew Arnold's 'Scholar Gypsy' and 'Thyrsis'. The tree stood not far from the village where the series was originally devised in 1971.

> *Roam on! The light we sought is shining still.*
> *Dost thou ask proof? Our tree yet crowns the hill,*
> *Our Scholar travels yet the loved hill-side*

from 'Thyrsis'

LEIGH HUNT

Selected Writings

Edited with an introduction by
DAVID JESSON-DIBLEY

ROUTLEDGE
New York

Published in USA and Canada in 2003 by
Routledge
29 West 35th Street
New York, NY 10001
www.routledge-ny.com

Routledge is an imprint of the Taylor & Francis Group.

By arrangement with Carcanet Press Ltd.

First published in Great Britain in 1990 by Carcanet Press Ltd

This impression 2003

Selection, introduction and editorial matter Copyright © David
Jesson-Dibley 1990, 2003

The right of David Jesson-Dibley to be identified as the editor of this
work has been asserted by him in accordance with the Copyright,
Designs and Patents Act of 1988

Cataloguing-in-Publication data is available from the Library of
Congress.
ISBN 0-415-96951-4

Printed and bound by SRP Limited, England

Contents

Biographical Introduction

James Leigh Hunt was born in Southgate on 19 October 1784 and died in Putney on 28 August 1859. He was named after James Henry Leigh, nephew of the 3rd Duke of Chandos, to whom his father, Isaac Hunt, a popular preacher, was a tutor.

Following eight years as a pupil at Christ's Hospital School in the City of London, and the publication of his *Juvenilia*, which his father saw through four editions, Leigh Hunt began a life-time career of journalism in 1805, making his precocious mark as a writer of theatrical criticism in *The News*, edited by his brother, John. In 1808, the brothers launched their best known weekly paper, *The Examiner*, with an editorial stance of liberal reform.

A year later, Hunt married Marianne Kent. Seven of their eleven children reached adulthood. Of these, the eldest, Thornton, published a collection of his father's letters after his death. The youngest, Vincent, Leigh Hunt's favourite, died seven years before his father at the age of thirty-one.

In 1813 and for the next two years, Hunt and his brother were obliged to edit *The Examiner* from separate gaols and to pay fines of £500 each for Hunt's alleged libel upon the Prince Regent. Hunt's wife and baby daughter were permitted to join him in Surrey gaol, where he seems to have been comfortably accommodated with wallpaper of his own choosing, his piano, and unlimited visits from admirers and friends, including Byron, Thomas Moore, Hazlitt and Lamb. Before his release he had written the greater part of his longest poem, *The Story of Rimini*, and a masque celebrating the downfall of Napoleon, *Descent of Liberty*.

The next three years were spent in Hampstead, where Hunt established his friendship with Shelley and Keats, commending their poetry to readers of *The Examiner* in 1816. In 1819, Hunt wrote a further appreciation of Keats's poetry for *The Indicator*, a weekly that Hunt sustained for a year and a half. In the same year, Shelley, of all Hunt's friends the most admired, dedicated *The Cenci* to him.

By 1821, the year in which Shelley and Byron invited him to Italy to launch a quarterly magazine, Hunt's reputation was at its peak amongst his own contemporaries, as poet, essayist, writer of political journalism, biographical sketches and literary criticism. His concern then, as throughout his career, was to refine the literary tastes of his readers, to cultivate their sensibilities and to extend their social sympathies. After a much delayed sea voyage, requiring Hunt and his family to winter in Plymouth, Hunt reached Leghorn on 1 July 1822, a week before Shelley was drowned.

The proposed quarterly, *The Liberal*, survived for four issues only. Relations between Hunt and Byron cooled and, after residing in Florence, in 1825 Hunt brought his family back to England and a series of lodgings in London. Eventually they settled in Upper Cheyne Row, Chelsea, where they were neighbours and friends of Thomas and Jane Carlyle from 1833 to 1840.

These were years of indigence and domestic disorder. Hunt was not in the best of health and his reputation had suffered through the publication of a candid appraisal of Byron, based on personal experience, in *Lord Byron and his Contemporaries*. Twenty years later, he was to stand by his myth-undermining observations, though conceding that their publication had been ill-timed.

Hunt's *Collected Poems* were published in 1832 and in 1844, the year in which he published his most substantial works of literary criticism, *Imagination and Fancy* and the essay, *What is Poetry?* By then he was almost at the end of his versatile though not very distinguished career as a poet. He had shown himself to be a modest innovator in narrative style with a commentator's keen eye for detail, a vigorous slapdash writer of burlesque and satire, a competent sonneteer, an easy exponent of conversational epistolary verse and an able translator of Greek, Roman, Italian and French poetry. In Rossetti's judgement, he was 'the greatest translator England had produced'. In addition, he had turned his hand to playwriting with *A Legend of Florence*, a verse drama staged with success at Covent Garden in 1840 and revived ten years later at Sadlers Wells and, by royal command, at Windsor

Castle. His late comedy, *Lover's Amazements*, was performed at the Lyceum in 1858, and seemed set for success, but the theatre went bankrupt.

In 1847 Hunt's domestic situation was relieved financially by the award of a pension of £200 a year, initiated by Lord John Russell, and the receipt of £440 raised by Charles Dickens and other friends, the profits of two public performances of Ben Jonson's *Everyman in his Humour*.

In prose, Hunt's later years were given over largely to his *Autobiography* (1850) and *The Religion of the Heart* (1853), the enlargement of earlier work to form a devotional handbook, which was widely read and valued. The *Autobiography*, Hunt's best known prose work, is an engagingly narrated memoir, the greater proportion of it dwelling upon his life prior to 1825.

The Hunts came to the last of their numerous residences in London – Cornwall Road, Hammersmith – in 1853, the year in which Vincent Hunt died and in which Hunt suffered the social embarrassment of identification with Henry Skimpole in Dickens's *Bleak House*. The breach was healed privately and three months after Hunt's death, Dickens made a public denial of intent in an article entitled *Leigh Hunt: A Remonstrance*. Marianne, who had been bedridden throughout her years in Hammersmith, died two years before her husband. During these last years, Hunt shared his home with two of his daughters and grandchildren. In 1859, he died peacefully in a friend's house in Putney at the age of seventy-five.

Though his talents were not of the highest order and were too widely dispersed, Hunt's unflagging commitment to humane social values and to the sharing of his literary insights and enthusiasms with receptive companions merit him the title of Ambassador Extraordinary of Literature during the first half of the nineteenth century. He outlived all the poets and essayists of his generation who, in reputation and distinctiveness, overshadowed him: Coleridge, Wordsworth, Byron, Shelley, Keats, Hazlitt, Lamb. But all owed a debt to his advocacy and editorial facility, as indeed did the leading poets of the next generation,

Tennyson and Browning. When, if ever, his letters are collected and published, the range of his interests and the warmth of his friendships will be more fully appreciated.

While writing for *The Indicator*, Hunt admitted: 'Hard is it for one who has grown up in the hope of being a poet, to confess that the best things he has done have been written in prose.' A modest conclusion and a sound one, though there is much pleasure to be had from his diverse poems. As for 'the best things' in his prose, not the least is his ready ability to share with his readers his enjoyment of literature and the pleasures of being alive. His aims were well summarized by his son, Thornton: 'To promote the happiness of his kind, to minister to the more educated appreciation of order and beauty, to open more widely the door of the library, and more widely the window of the library looking out upon nature, – these were the purposes that guided his studies and animated his labour to the very last.'

In literature, he holds a unique if not outstanding place as poet, critic, translator, journalist, essayist, anthologist and mediator to his reading public of literary values, enthusiasms and taste.

Select Bibliography

1801	*Juvenilia;* or, a Collection of Poems (3rd edn. 1802, 4th edn. 1803)
1816	*The Story of Rimini,* a Poem (3rd edn. 1819)
1819	*The Poetical Works of Leigh Hunt* (further volumes 1832, 1844, 1862)
1818	*Lord Byron and Some of His Contemporaries;* with Recollections of the Author's Life, and of his Visit to Italy
1835	*Captain Sword and Captain Pen,* a Poem (2nd edn. 1839, 3rd edn. 1849)
1840	*A Legend of Florence.* A Play. In Five Acts.
1844	*Imagination and Fancy;* or Selections from the English Poets...and an Essay in answer to the Question 'What is Poetry?'
1850	*The Autobiography of Leigh Hunt;* with Reminiscences of Friends and Contemporaries. 3 vols.
1851	*Table Talk* To which are added Imaginary Conversations of Pope and Swift
1853	*The Religion of the Heart.* A Manual of Faith and Duty.
1857	*The Prose Works of Leigh Hunt* 4 vols. American edn.
1862	*The Correspondence of Leigh Hunt* Edited by his Eldest Son. 2 vols.

Some periodicals edited by Hunt:

1808-21	*The Examiner,* a Sunday Paper
1819-21	*The Indicator.* Weekly
1822-23	*The Liberal.* 4 Nos.
1830-32	*The Tatler* a Daily Journal of Literature and the Stage
1850-51	*Leigh Hunt's Journal.* Weekly

Recent Editions:

1891 *Essays and Poems*
     ed. R.B. Johnson
1923 *The Poetical Works of Leigh Hunt*
     ed. H.S. Milford
1949 *The Autobiography of Leigh Hunt*
     ed. J.E. Morpurgo
1949 *Leigh Hunt's Dramatic Criticism*
     eds. Lawrence H. & Carolyn W. Houtchens
1956 *Leigh Hunt's Literary Criticism*
     eds. Lawrence H. & Carolyn W. Houtchens
1959 *Leigh Hunt's Autobiography: the earliest sketches*
     ed. Stephen F. Fogle
1962 *Leigh Hunt's Political and Occasional Essays*
     eds. Lawrence H. & Carolyn W. Houtchens

Biography:

1930 *Leigh Hunt and His Circle*
     Edmund Blunden
1985 *Immortal Boy, a Portrait of Leigh Hunt*
     Ann Blainey

Selection from Leigh Hunt's *Autobiography*, his most substantial prose work, has been limited here, as it merits either a reissue of Professor Morpurgo's edition of 1949 (Cresset Press, London), or a fresh one.

From the Preface to *The Story of Rimini*

Poetry, in its highest sense, belongs exclusively to such men as Shakspeare, Spenser, and others, who possessed the deepest insight into the spirit and sympathies of all things; but poetry, in the most comprehensive application of the term, I take to be the flower of any kind of experience, rooted in truth, and issuing forth into beauty. All that the critic has a right to demand of it, according to its degree, is, that it should spring out of a real impulse, be consistent in its parts, and shaped into some characteristic harmony of verse. Without these requisites (apart from fleeting and artificial causes), the world will scarcely look at any poetical production a second time; whereas, if it possess them, the humblest poetry stands a chance of surviving not only whatever is falsely so called, but much that contains, here and there, more poetical passages than itself; passages that are the fits and starts of a fancy without judgment – the incoherences of a nature, poetical only by convulsion, but prosaic in its ordinary strength.

Thus, in their several kinds, we have the poetry of thought and passion in Shakspeare and Chaucer; of poetical abstraction and enjoyment in Spenser; of scholarship and a rapt ambition in Milton; of courtliness in Waller (who writes like an inspired gentleman-usher); of gallantry in Suckling; of wit and satire in Pope; of heartiness in Burns; of the 'fat of the land' in Thomson; of a certain sequestered gentleness in Shenstone; and the poetry of prose itself in Dryden: not that he was a prosaic writer; but that what other people thought in prose, he could think in verse; and so made absolute poems of pamphlets and party-reasoning.

The first quality of a poet is imagination, or that faculty by which the subtlest idea is given us of the nature or condition of any one thing, by illustration from another, or by the inclusion of remote affinities: as when Shakspeare speaks of moonlight *sleeping* on a bank; or of nice customs *curtseying* to great kings (though the reader may, if he pleases, put this under the head of wit, or imagination in miniature); or where Milton speaks of towers *bosom'd* in trees, or of motes that *people* the sunbeams; or

13

compares Satan on the wing at a distance, to a fleet of ships *hanging* in the clouds; or where Mr. Shelley (for I avoid quoting from living writers, lest it should be thought invidious towards such as are not quoted) puts that stately, superior, and comprehensive image, into the mouth of a speaker who is at once firm of soul, and yet anticipates a dreadful necessity –

'I see, *as from a tower*, the *end of all:*'

or lastly, where Mr Keats tells us of the *realmless eyes* of old Saturn (as he sits musing after his dethronement); or of the two brothers and *their murdered man*, riding from Florence; that is to say, the man whom they were *about* to murder; or where, by one exquisite touch, he describes an important and affecting office of the god Mercury, and the effects of it upon the spectators in the lower world – calling him 'the *star* of Lethe;' by which we see that he was the only bright object which visited that dreary region. We behold him rising on its borders.

In proportion to the imagination, is the abstract poetical faculty: in proportion to extent of sympathy (for passion, which is everywhere in poetry, may be comparatively narrow and self-revolving), is the power of universality: in proportion to energy of temperament and variety of experience, is the power of embodying the conceptions in a greater or less amount of consistent and stirring action, whether narrative or dramatic. The greatest poets have the greatest amount of all these qualities conjoined: the next greatest are those who unite the first two: the next, those whose imagination is exquisite as far as it goes, but is confined to certain spheres of contemplation: then come the poets, who have less imagination, but more action – who are imaginative, as it were, in the mass, and with a certain vague enjoyment allied to the feelings of youth: then the purely artificial poets, or such as poetize in art rather than nature, or upon conventional beauty and propriety, as distinguished from beauty universal: and then follow the minor wits, the song-writers, burlesquers, &c. In every instance, the indispensable requisites are truth of feeling, freedom from superfluity (that is, the absence of forced or unfitting thoughts), and beauty of result; and in proportion as these requisites are comprehensive, profound, and active, the poet is great. But it is always to be borne in mind, that the writers in any of these classes, who take lasting hold of the world's attention, are justly accounted superior to such as afford less evidences of power in a higher class. The pretension is nothing; the performance every thing. A good apple is better than an insipid peach. A song of Burns is (literally) worth half the poets in the collections.

Suckling's *Ballad on a Wedding* is a small and unambitious, yet unmisgiving and happy production, of no rank whatsoever considered with reference to the height of poetry; but so excellent of its kind for consistency, freshness, and relish, that it has survived hundreds of epithalamiums, and epics too; and will last as long as beauty has a lip, or gallantry frankness.

Shenstone's *School-mistress* is a poem of a very humble description in subject, style, and everything, except its humane and thoughtful sweetness: yet being founded in truth, and consistent, and desiring nothing but truth and consistency, it has survived in like manner. Compared with greater productions, it resembles the herbs which the author speaks of in its cottage-garden; but balm and mint have their flourishing, as well as the aloe; and like them, and its old heroine, it has secured its 'grey renown,' clean as her mob-cap, and laid up in lavender. Crashaw is a poet now scarcely known except to book-worms. Pope said of him, that his writing was 'a mixture of tender gentle thoughts and suitable expressions, of forced and inextricable conceits, and of needless fillers-up to the rest.' Crashaw had a morbid enthusiasm, which sometimes helped him to an apprehensiveness and depth of expression, perhaps beyond the voluntary power of his great critic; yet Pope, by writing nothing out of what the painters call 'keeping', or unworthy of himself, is justly reckoned worth a hundred Crashaws. Random thoughts and fillings-up are a poet's *felo de se*.

Far am I, in making these remarks, from pretending to claim any part or parcel in the fellowship of names consecrated by time. I can truly say, that, except when I look upon some others that get into the collections, consecrated by no hands but the book-

15

jobbers, I do not know (after I have written them) whether my verses deserve to live a dozen days longer. The confession may be thought strong or weak, as it happens; but such is the fact. I have witnessed so much self-delusion in my time, and partaken of so much, and the older I grow, my veneration so increases for poetry not to be questioned, that all I can be sure of, is my admiration of genius in others. I cannot say how far I overvalue it, or even undervalue it, in myself. I am in the condition of a lover who is sure that he loves, and is therefore happy in the presence of the beloved object; but is uncertain how far he is worthy to be beloved. Perhaps the symptom is a bad one, and only better than that of a confident ignorance. Perhaps the many struggles of my life; the strange conflicting thoughts upon a thousand matters, into which I have been forced; the necessity of cultivating some modesty of self-knowledge, as a set-off to peremptoriness of public action; and the unceasing alternation of a melancholy and a cheerfulness, equally native to my blood – and the latter of which I have suffered to go its lengths, both as an innocent propensity and a means of resistance – have combined in me to baffle conclusion, and filled me full of these *perhapses*, which I have observed growing upon my writings for many years past. *Perhaps* the question is not worth a word I have said of it, except upon that principle of 'gossiping' with which my preface sets out, and which I hope will procure me the reader's pardon for starting it. All that I was going to say was, that if I cannot do in poetry what ought to be done, I know what ought not; and that if there is no truth in my verses, I look for no indulgence...

...I took up the subject of the *Story of Rimini* at one of the happiest periods of my life; otherwise I confess I should have chosen a less melancholy one. Not that melancholy subjects are unpopular, or that pain, for any great purpose, is to be avoided; much less so sweet a one as that of pity. I am apt enough to think, with the poet's good-natured title to his play, that 'All's well that ends well'; and am as willing as any man to bear my share of suffering, for the purpose of bringing about that moral to human story. My life has been half made up of the effort.

Neither is every tragical subject so melancholy as the word might be supposed to imply; for not to mention those balms of beauty and humanity with which great poets reconcile the sharpest wounds they give us, there are stories (*Hero and Leander* is one of them), in which the persons concerned are so innocent, and appear to have been happy for so long a time, that the most distressing termination of their felicity hardly hinders a secret conviction, that they might well suffer bitterly for so short a one. Their tragedy is the termination of happiness, and not the consummation of misery.

But besides the tendency I have from animal spirits, as well as from need of comfort, to indulge my fancy in happier subjects, it appears to me, that the world has become experienced enough to be capable of receiving its best profit through the medium of pleasurable, instead of painful, appeals to its reflection. There is an old philosophic conviction reviving among us as a popular one (and there could not be one more desirable), that it is time for those who would benefit their species, to put an end to recriminations, and denouncements, and threats, and agree to consider the sufferings of mankind as arising out of want of knowledge rather than defect of goodness, – as intimations which, like the physical pain of a wound, or a galling ligament, tell us that we are to set about removing the causes of pain, instead of venting the spleen of it.

Agreeably to this conviction, and to the good-nature of it, it appears desirable, that tragical stories should be so written, as to leave no chance of misconception with regard to the first discernible causes of the error that produced the tragedy. Now what is this first cause in the story which stands at the head of the present volume? Is it the crime committed by the father, in entrapping his daughter into a marriage unfit for her? No: it is not even that. It is the habit of falsehood which pervaded society around him, and which therefore enabled and encouraged him to lie for that purpose: in other words, it was the great social mistake, still the commonest among us, arising from want of better knowledge, and producing endless mistake, confusion, and a war of principle, in all the relations of life. Society lied, and taught lying, with contradictory tenets that drove the habit to desperation; and then, with the natural anger of inconvenienced folly, and after the fashion of the brute beasts we read of, who sit clawing their wounds, it took the last guilty sufferer for the first: and this it has been doing, more or less, ever since half-knowledge took itself for whole, or a partial perception of its ignorance exasperated and degraded it into spleen and bigotry. A secret uneasiness has accordingly pervaded all moral criticism, especially where the critic has not been wanting in a good measure of natural benevolence; nay, where the temperament has been violent, and the will greater than the reason, it has sometimes exasperated him and made him inhuman, in proportion to his very desire of sympathy. I remember I was never more astonished, than when some of the critics of the poem in question (not altogether impartial, however, on the political score), found out, that the hero and heroine had not suffered enough for the cause of good morals, and that they were too amiable! What would such critics have? Is it the unamiable alone who suffer, or who require to be warned against the perils they undergo? Or is it none but the amiable who are weak and thoughtless? Or must the cruellest temptations into which duplicity and error can bring people, be kept out of sight, purely to please the morbid fancies and social bad consciences of those who perpetuate them? Lastly, I would ask, whether a long train of misery, and a tragical death, are no calamities, or 'nothing to speak of'? I cannot answer, either for the misgivings of false morals, or for the strange fascinations of those, who might choose, for aught I know, to go and disobey their parents, and take to drinking poison, because last night they had seen the play of *Romeo and Juliet*, or the *Orphan*! But this I know, that I thought the catastrophe a very dreadful one when I wrote it, and the previous misery still worse; and that although I certainly intended no moral lesson, or thought about it, when I was led by the perusal of the story in Dante to attempt making a book of it, the subject gradually forced upon me the consideration of those first causes of error, of which I have been speaking.

I thought of putting for a motto to the second edition, a passage out of the *Orlando Innamorato*:

'Bisogna ben guardare
Al primo errore, ed inconveniente.'

'Guard well against the first, unfit mistake.'

But so little did I suspect that any one could remain unimpressed with the catastrophe, that I doubted whether the motto itself would not be mixed up too exclusively with the principal sufferers. I am glad to think it is now likely to be otherwise, and that to those who choose to reflect on the tragedy of Dante's story, no link in the chain of moral causes need be lost sight of. It would be idle to reply, that, by bringing out a first cause, we cease to absorb attention upon the second, and endanger a just dread of it. Society only becomes the more bound to see into that first evil, without the existence of which we should not have so many others.

It is a great pleasure to me to reflect, that, before I had become aware of the inestimable value of the love of truth, as the foundation of every thing finally good, in poetry, philosophy, and the government of the world, I had unconsciously been giving a lesson upon it in a poetical form... 1832

The Story of Rimini[1]

Time, the close of the thirteenth century; –
Scene, first at Ravenna, afterwards at Rimini

CANTO I
The coming to fetch the Bride from Ravenna

The sun is up, and 'tis a morn of May
Round old Ravenna's clear-shewn towers and bay,
A morn, the loveliest which the year has seen,
Last of the spring, yet fresh with all its green;

For a warm eve, and gentle rains at night,
Have left a sparkling welcome for the light,
And there's a crystal clearness all about;
The leaves are sharp, the distant hills look out;
A balmy briskness comes upon the breeze;
The smoke goes dancing from the cottage trees; 10
And when you listen, you may hear a coil
Of bubbling springs about the grassy soil;
And all the scene, in short – sky, earth and sea,
Breathes like a bright-eyed face, that laughs out openly.

'Tis nature, full of spirits, waked and springing: –
The birds to the delicious time are singing,
Darting with freaks and snatches up and down,
Where the light woods go seaward from the town;
While happy faces, striking through the green
Of leafy roads, at every turn are seen; 20
And the far ships, lifting their sails of white
Like joyful hands, come up with scattery light,
Come gleaming up, true to the wished-for day,
And chase the whistling brine, and swirl into the bay.

And well may all who can, come crowding there,
If peace returning, and processions rare,
And to crown all, a marriage in May weather,
Have aught to bring enjoying hearts together;
For on this sparkling day, Ravenna's pride,
The daughter of their prince, becomes a bride, 30
A bride, to crown the comfort of the land:
And he, whose victories have obtained her hand,
Has taken with the dawn, so flies report,
His promised journey to the expecting court
With hasting pomp, and squires of high degree,
The bold Giovanni, lord of Rimini.

Already in the streets the stir grows loud

20

Of expectation and a bustling crowd.
With feet and voice the gathering hum contends,
The deep talk heaves, the ready laugh ascends: 40
Callings, and clapping doors, and curs unite,
And shouts from mere exuberance of delight,
And armed bands, making important way,
Gallant and grave, the lords of holiday,
And nodding neighbours, greeting as they run,
And pilgrims, chanting in the morning sun.
With heaved-out tapestry the windows glow,
By lovely faces brought, that come and go;
Till, the work smoothed, and all the street attired,
They take their seats, with upward gaze admired;   50
Some looking down, some forwards or aside,
As suits the conscious charm in which they pride;
Some turning a trim waist, or o'er the flow
Of crimson cloths hanging a hand of snow;
But all with smiles prepared, and garlands green,
And all in fluttering talk, impatient for the scene.

And hark! the approaching trumpets, with a start,
On the smooth wind come dancing to the heart.
A moment's hush succeeds; and from the walls,
Firm and at once, a silver answer calls,   60
Then heave the crowd; and all, who best can strive
In shuffling struggle, tow'rd the palace drive,
Where balconied and broad, of marble fair,
On pillars it o'erlooks the public square;
For there Duke Guido is to hold his state
With his fair daughter, seated o'er the gate: –
But the full place rejects the invading tide;
And after a rude heave from side to side,
With angry faces turned, and feet regained,
The peaceful press with order is maintained,   70
Leaving the door-ways only for the crowd,
The space within for the procession proud.

For in this manner is the square set out: –
The sides, path-deep, are crowded round about,
And faced with guards, who keep the road entire;
And opposite to these a brilliant quire
Of knights and ladies hold the central spot,
Seated in groups upon a grassy plot;
The seats with boughs are shaded from above
Of early trees transplanted from a grove,   80
And in the midst, fresh whistling through the scene,
A lightsome fountain starts from out the green,
Clear and compact, till, at its height o'er-run,
It shakes its loosening silver in the sun.

There, talking with the ladies, you may see,
Standing about, or seated, frank and free,
Some of the finest warriors of the court, –
Baptist, and Hugo of the princely port,
And Azo, and Obizo, and the grace
Of frank Esmeriald with his open face,   90
And Felix the Fine Arm, and him who well
Repays his lavish honours, Lionel,
Besides a host of spirits, nursed in glory,
Fit for sweet woman's love and for the poet's story.

There too, in thickest of the bright-eyed throng,
Stands the young father of Italian song,
Guy Cavalcanti, of a knightly race;
The poet looks out in his earnest face;
He with the pheasant's plume – there – bending now,
Something he speaks around him with a bow,   100
And all the listening looks, with nods and flushes,
Breaks round him into smiles and sparkling blushes.

Another start of trumpets, with reply;
And o'er the gate a sudden canopy
Raises, on ivory shafts, a crimson shade,

22

And Guido issues with the princely maid,
And sits; – the courtiers fall on either side;
But every look is fixed upon the bride,
Who pensive comes at first, and hardly hears
The enormous shout that springs as she appears,   110
Till, as she views the countless gaze below,
And faces that with grateful homage glow,
A home to leave, and husband yet to see,
Fade in the warmth of that great charity;
And hard it is, she thinks, to have no will;
But not to bless these thousands, harder still:
With that, a keen and quivering glance of tears
Scarce moves her patient mouth, and disappears;
A smile is underneath, and breaks away,
And round she looks and breathes, as best befits the day.   120

What need I tell of lovely lips and eyes,
A clipsome waist, and bosom's balmy rise,
The dress of bridal white, and the dark curls
Bedding an airy coronet of pearls?
There's not in all that crowd one gallant being,
Whom if his heart were whole, and rank agreeing,
It would not fire to twice of what he is,
To clasp her to his heart, and call her his.

While thus with tip-toe looks the people gaze,
Another shout the neighb'ring quarters raise: 130
The train are in the town, and gathering near,
With noise of cavalry, and trumpets clear;
A princely music, unbedinned with drums:
The mighty brass seems opening as it comes,
And now it fills, and now it shakes the air,
And now it bursts into the sounding square;
At which the crowd with such a shout rejoice,
Each thinks he's deafened with his neighbour's voice.
Then, with a long-drawn breath, the clangours die;

23

The palace trumpets give a last reply,   140
And clattering hoofs succeed, with stately stir
Of snortings proud and clinking furniture:
It seems as if the harnessed war were near;
But in their garb of peace the train appear,
Their swords alone reserved, but idly hung,
And the chains freed by which their shields were slung.

First come the trumpeters, clad all in white
Except the breast, which wears a scutcheon bright.
By four and four they ride, on horses grey;
And as they sit along their easy way,   150
Stately, and heaving to the sway below,
Each plants his trumpet on his saddle-bow.

The heralds next appear, in vests attired
Of stiffening gold with radiant colours fired;
And then the pursuivants, who wait on these,
All dressed in painted richness to the knees:
Each rides a dappled horse, and bears a shield,
Charged with three heads upon a golden field.

Twelve ranks of squires come after, twelve in one,
With forked pennons lifted in the sun,   160
Which tell, as they look backward in the wind,
The bearings of the knights that ride behind.
Their steeds are ruddy bay; and every squire
His master's colour shews in his attire.
These past, and at a lordly distance, come
The knights themselves, and fill the quickening hum,
The flower of Rimini. Apart they ride,
Six in a row, and with a various pride;
But all as fresh as fancy could desire,
All shapes of gallantry on steeds of fire.   170

Differing in colours is the knights' array

The horses, black and chestnut, roan and bay; –
The horsemen, crimson vested, purple, and white, –
All but the scarlet cloak for every knight,
Which thrown apart, and hanging loose behind,
Rests on his steed, and ruffles in the wind.
Their caps of velvet have a lightsome fit,
Each with a dancing feather sweeping it,
Tumbling its white against their short dark hair;
But what is of the most accomplished air,   180
All wear memorials of their lady's love,
A ribbon, or a scarf, or silken glove,
Some tied about their arm, some at the breast,
Some, with a drag, dangling from the cap's crest.

A suitable attire the horses shew;
Their golden bits keep wrangling as they go;
The bridles glance about with gold and gems;
And the rich housing-cloths, above the hems
Which comb along the ground with golden pegs,
Are half of net, to shew the hinder legs.   190
Some of the cloths themselves are golden thread
With silk enwoven, azure, green, or red;
Some spotted on a ground of different hue,
As burning stars upon a cloth of blue, –
Or purple smearings with a velvet light
Rich from the glary yellow thickening bright, –
Or a spring green, powdered with April posies, –
Or flush vermilion, set with silver roses:
But all are wide and large, and with the wind,
When it comes fresh, go sweeping out behind.   200
With various earnestness the crowd admire
Horsemen and horse, the motion and the attire.
Some watch, as they go by, the riders' faces
Looking composure, and their knightly graces;
The life, the carelessness, the sudden heed,
The body curving to the rearing steed,

The patting hand, that best persuades the check,
And makes the quarrel up with a proud neck,
The thigh broad pressed, the spanning palm upon it,
And the jerked feather swaling in the bonnet.   210

Others the horses and their pride explore,
Their jauntiness behind and strength before;
The flowing back, firm chest, and fetlocks clean,
The branching veins ridging the glossy lean,
The mane hung sleekly, the projecting eye
That to the stander near looks awfully,
The finished head, in its compactness free,
Small, and o'erarching to the lifted knee,
The start and snatch, as if they felt the comb,
With mouths that fling about the creamy foam,   220
The snorting turbulence, the nod, the champing,
The shift, the tossing, and the fiery tramping.

And now the Princess, pale and with fixed eye,
Perceives the last of those precursors nigh,
Each rank uncovering, as they pass in state,
Both to the courtly fountain and the gate.
And then a second interval succeeds
Of stately length, and then a troop of steeds
Milkwhite and unattired, Arabian bred,
Each by a blooming boy lightsomely led: 230
In every limb is seen their faultless race,
A fire well tempered, and a free left grace:
Slender their spotless shapes, and meet the sight
With freshness, after all those colours bright:
And as with quoit-like drop their steps they bear,
They lend their streaming tails to the fond air.
These for a princely present are divined,
And shew the giver is not far behind.

The talk increases now, and now advance,

26

Space after space, with many a sprightly prance,   240
The pages of the court, in rows of three;
Of white and crimson is their livery.
Space after space, – and yet the attendants come, –
And deeper goes about the impatient hum –
Ah – yes – no – 'tis not he – but 'tis the squires
Who go before him when his pomp requires;
And now his huntsman shews the lessening train,
Now the squire-carver, and the chamberlain, –
And now his banner comes, and now his shield
Borne by the squire that waits him to the field, –   250
And then an interval, – a lordly space; –
A pin-drop silence strikes o'er all the place;
The princess, from a distance, scarcely knows
Which way to look; her colour comes and goes;
And with an impulse and affection free
She lays her hand upon her father's knee,
Who looks upon her with a laboured smile,
Gathering it up into his own the while,
When some one's voice, as if it knew not how
To check itself, exclaims, 'the prince! now – now!'   260
And on a milk-white courser, like the air,
A glorious figure springs into the square;
Up, with a burst of thunder, goes the shout,
And rolls the trembling walls and peopled roofs about.

Never was nobler finish of fine sight;
'Twas like the coming of a shape of light;
And every lovely gazer, with a start,
Felt the quick pleasure smite across her heart: –
The princess, who at first could scarcely see,
Though looking still that way from dignity,   270
Gathers new courage as the praise goes round,
And bends her eyes to learn what they have found.
And see, – his horse obeys the check unseen;
And with an air 'twixt ardent and serene,

27

Letting a fall of curls about his brow,
He takes his cap off with a gallant bow;
Then for another and a deafening shout;
And scarfs are waved, and flowers come fluttering out;
And, shaken by the noise, the reeling air
Sweeps with a giddy whirl among the fair,   280
And whisks their garments, and their shining hair.

With busy interchange of wonder glows
The crowd, and loves his brilliance as he goes, –
The golden-fretted cap, the downward feather, –
The crimson vest fitting with pearls together, –
The rest in snowy white from the mid thigh:
These catch the extrinsic and the common eye:
But on his shape the gentler sight attends,
Moves as he passes, – as he bends him, bends, –
Watches his air, his gesture, and his face,   290
And thinks it never saw such manly grace,
So fine are his bare throat, and curls of black, –
So lightsomely dropt in, his lordly back –
His thigh so fitted for the tilt or dance,
So heaped with strength, and turned with elegance;
But above all, so meaning is his look, ·
Full, and as readable as open book;
And so much easy dignity there lies
In the frank lifting of his cordial eyes.

His haughty steed, who seems by turns to be   300
Vexed and made proud by that cool mastery,
Shakes at his bit, and rolls his eyes with care,
Reaching with stately step at the fine air;
And now and then, sideling his restless pace,
Drops with his hinder legs, and shifts his place,
And feels through all his frame a fiery thrill:
The princely rider on his back sits still,
And looks where'er he likes, and sways him at his will.

Surprise, relief, a joy scarce understood,
Something perhaps of very gratitude,   310
And fifty feelings, undefined and new,
Dance through the bride, and flush her faded hue.
'Could I but once', she thinks, 'securely place
A trust for the contents on such a case,
And know the spirit that should fill that dwelling,
This chance of mine would hardly be compelling.'
Just then, the stranger, coming slowly round
By the clear fountain and the brilliant ground,
And bending, as he goes, with frequent thanks,
Beckons a follower to him from the ranks,   320
And loosening, as he speaks, from its light hold
A dropping jewel with its chain of gold,
Sends it, in token he had loved him long,
To the young father of Italian song:
The youth smiles up, and with a lowly grace
Bending his lifted eyes and blushing face,
Looks after his new friend, who, scarcely gone
In the wide turning, nods and passes on.

This is sufficient for the destined bride;
She took an interest first, but now a pride;   330
And as the prince comes riding to the place,
Baring his head, and raising his fine face,
She meets his full obeisance with an eye
Of self-permission and sweet gravity;
He looks with touched respect, and gazes, and goes by.

CANTO II
The Bride's Journey to Rimini

We'll pass the followers, and their closing state;
The court was entered by a hinder gate;
The duke and princess had retired before,

29

Joined by the knights and ladies at the door;
But something seemed amiss, and there ensued
Deep talk among the spreading multitude,
Who got in clumps, or paced the measured street,
Filling with earnest hum the noontide heat;
Nor ceased the wonder, as the day increased,
And brought no symptoms of a bridal feast,   10
No mass, no tilt, no largess for the crowd,
Nothing to answer that procession proud;
But a blank look, as if no court had been;
Silence without, and secrecy within;
And nothing heard by listening at the walls,
But now and then a bustling through the halls,
Or the dim organ roused at gathering intervals.

The truth was this: – The bridegroom had not come,
But sent his brother, proxy in his room.
A lofty spirit the former was, and proud,   20
Little gallant, and had a sort of cloud
Hanging for ever on his cold address,
Which he mistook for proper manliness.
But more of this hereafter. Guido knew
The prince's character; and he knew too,
That sweet as was his daughter, and prepared
To do her duty, where appeal was barred,
She had stout notions on the marrying score,
And where the match unequal prospect bore,
Might pause with firmness, and refuse to strike   30
A chord her own sweet music so unlike.
The old man therefore, kind enough at heart,
Yet fond from habit of intrigue and art,
And little formed for sentiments like these,
Which seemed to him mere maiden niceties,
Had thought at once to gratify the pride
Of his stern neighbour, and secure the bride,
By telling him, that if, as he had heard,

Busy he was just then, 'twas but a word,
And he might send and wed her by another, –   40
Of course, no less a person than his brother.
The bride meantime was told, and not unmoved,
To look for one no sooner seen than loved;
And when Giovanni, struck with what he thought
Mere proof how his triumphant hand was sought,
Dispatched the wished for prince, who was a creature
Formed in the very poetry of nature,
The effect was perfect, and the future wife
Caught in the elaborate snare, perhaps for life.

One shock there was, however, to sustain,   50
Which nigh restored her to herself again.
She saw, when all were housed, in Guido's face
A look of leisurely surprise take place;
A little whispering followed for a while,
And then 'twas told her with an easy smile,
That Prince Giovanni, to his great chagrin,
Had been delayed by something unforeseen,
But rather than defer his day of bliss
(If his fair ruler took it not amiss)
Had sent his brother Paulo in his stead;   60
'Who', said old Guido, with a nodding head,
'May well be said to represent his brother,
For when you see the one, you know the other.'

By this time Paulo joined them where they stood,
And, seeing her in some uneasy mood,
Changed the mere cold respects his brother sent
To such a strain of cordial compliment,
And paid them with an air so frank and bright,
As to a friend appreciated at sight,
That air, in short which sets you at your ease,   70
Without implying your perplexities,
That what with the surprise in every way,

31

The hurry of the time, the appointed day,
The very shame which now appeared increased,
Of begging leave to have her hand released,
And above all, those tones, and smiles, and looks,
Which seemed to realize the dreams of books
And helped her genial fancy to conclude
That fruit of such a stock must all be good,
She knew not how to object in her confusion;   80
Quick were the marriage-rites; and, in conclusion,
The proxy, turning midst the general hush,
Kissed her meek lips, betwixt a rosy blush.

At last, about the vesper hour, a score
Of trumpets issued from the palace door,
The banners of their brass with favours tied,
And with a blast proclaimed the wedded bride.
But not a word the sullen silence broke,
Till something of a gift the herald spoke,
And with a bag of money issuing out,   90
Scattered the ready harvest round about;
Then burst the mob into a jovial cry,
And largess! largess! claps against the sky,
And bold Giovanni's name, the lord of Rimini.

The rest however still were looking on,
Careless and mute, and scarce the noise was gone,
When riding from the gate, with banners reared,
Again the morning visitors appeared.
The prince was in his place; and in a car,
Before him, glistening like a farewell star,   100
Sate the dear lady with her brimming eyes;
And off they set, through doubtful looks and cries;
For some too shrewdly guessed, and some were vexed
At the dull day, and some the whole perplexed;
And all great pity thought it to divide
Two that seemed made for bridegroom and for bride.

Ev'n she, whose heart this strange, abrupt event
Had seared, as 'twere, a passionate cry forbear
At leaving her own home and native air; 110
Till passing now the limits of the town,
And on the last few gazers looking down,
She saw by the road-side an aged throng,
Who wanting power to bustle with the strong,
Had learnt their gracious mistress was to go,
And gathered there, an unconcerted shew;
Bending they stood, with their old foreheads bare,
And the winds fingered with their reverend hair.
Farewell! farewell, my friends! she would have cried,
But in her throat the leaping accents died, 120
And, waving with her hand a vain adieu,
She dropt her veil, and backwarder withdrew
And let the kindly tears their own good course pursue.

It was a lovely evening, fit to close
A lovely day, and brilliant in repose.
Warm, but not dim, a glow was in the air;
The softened breeze came smoothing here and there;
And every tree, in passing, one by one,
Gleamed out with twinkles of the golden sun:
For leafy was the road, with tall array, 130
On either side, of mulberry and bay,
And distant snatches of blue hills between;
And there the alder was with its bright green,
And the broad chestnut, and the poplar's shoot,
That like a feather waves from head to foot,
With, ever and anon, majestic pines;
And still from tree to tree the early vines
Hung garlanding the way in amber lines.

Nor long the princess kept her from the view
Of that dear scenery with its parting hue: 140
For sitting now, calm from the gush of tears,

With dreaming eye fixed down, and half-shut ears,
Hearing, yet hearing not, the fervent sound
Of hoofs thick reckoning and the wheel's moist round,
A call of 'slower!' from the farther part
Of the checked riders, woke her with a start;
And looking up again, half sigh, half stare,
She lifts her veil, and feels the freshening air.

'Tis down a hill they go, gentle indeed,
And such, as with a bold and pranksome speed   150
Another time they would have scorned to measure;
But now they take with them a lovely treasure,
And feel they should consult her gentle pleasure.

And now with thicker shades the pines appear;
The noise of hoofs grows duller to her ear;
And quitting suddenly their gravelly toil,
The wheels go spinning o'er a sandy soil.
Here first the silence of the country seems
To come about her with its listening dreams,
And, full of anxious thoughts, half freed from pain,   160
In downward musing she relapsed again,
Leaving the others who had passed that way
In careless spirits of the early day,
To look about, and mark the reverend scene,
For awful tales renowned, and everlasting green.

A heavy spot the forest looks at first,
To one grim shade condemned, and sandy thirst,
Or only chequered, here and there, with bushes
Dusty and sharp, or plashy pools with rushes,
About whose sides the swarming insects fry,   170
Opening with noisome din, as they go by.
But entering more and more, they quit the sand
At once, and strike upon a grassy land,
From which the trees, as from a carpet, rise

In knolls and clumps, with rich varieties.
A moment's trouble find the knights to rein
Their horses in, which, feeling turf again,
Thrill, and curvet, and long to be at large
To scour the space and give the winds a charge,
Or pulling tight the bridles, as they pass,   180
Dip their warm mouths into the freshening grass.
But soon in easy rank, from glade to glade,
Proceed they, coasting underneath the shade,
Some baring to the cool their placid brows,
Some looking upward through the glimmering boughs,
Or peering grave through inward-opening places,
And half prepared for glimpse of shadowy faces.
Various the trees and passing foliage here, –
Wild pear, and oak, and dusky juniper,
With briony between in trails of white,   190
And ivy, and the suckle's streaky light,
And moss, warm gleaming with a sudden mark,
Like flings of sunshine left upon the bark,
And still the pine, long-haired, and dark, and tall,
In lordly right, predominant o'er all.

Much they admire that old religious tree
With shaft above the rest up-shooting free,
And shaking, when its dark locks feel the wind,
Its wealthy fruit with rough Mosaic rind.
At noisy intervals, the living cloud   200
Of cawing rooks breaks o'er them, gathering loud
Like a wild people at a stranger's coming;
Then hushing paths succeed, with insects humming,
Or ring-dove, that repeats his pensive plea,
Or startled gull, up-screaming tow'rds the sea.
But scarce their eyes encounter living thing,
Save, now and then, a goat loose wandering,
Or a few cattle, looking up aslant
With sleepy eyes and meek mouths ruminant;

Or once, a plodding woodman, old and bent,   210
Passing with half-indifferent wonderment,
Yet turning, at the last, to look once more;
Then feels his trembling staff, and onward as before.

So ride they pleased, – till now the couching sun
Levels his final look through shadows dun;
And the clear moon, with meek o'er-lifted face,
Seems come to look into the silvering place.
Then first the bride waked up, for then was heard,
Sole voice, the poet's and the lover's bird,
Preluding first, as if the sounds were cast   220
For the dear leaves about her, till at last
With shot-out raptures, in a perfect shower,
She vents her heart on the delicious hour.
Lightly the horsemen go, as if they'd ride
A velvet path, and hear no voice beside:
A placid hope assures the breath-suspended bride.

So ride they in delight through beam and shade; –
Till many a rill now passed, and many a glade,
They quit the piny labyrinths, and soon
Emerge into the full and sheeted moon: 230
Chilling it seems; and pushing steed on steed,
They start them freshly with a homeward speed.
Then well-known fields they pass, and straggling cots,
Boy-storied trees, and passion-plighted spots;
And turning last a sudden corner, see
The square-lit towers of slumbering Rimini.
The marble bridge comes heaving forth below
With a long gleam; and nearer as they go,
They see the still Marecchia, cold and bright,
Sleeping along with face against the light.   240
A hollow trample now, – a fall of chains, –
The bride has entered, – not a voice remains; –
Night, and a maiden silence, wrap the plains.

From CANTO III
The Fatal Passion

(The brothers are contrasted. Both are fine horsemen, but Giovanni has a prouder and more martial disposition than Paulo, whose finer and tenderer sensibilities soon stir the heart of the dutiful bride. Unspoken love draws Paulo increasingly into the company of Francesca, while Giovanni, unconcerned, goes about his public affairs.)

. Francesca from herself but ill could hide
What pleasure now was added to her side, –
How placidly, yet fast, the days succeeded
With one who thought and felt so much as she did, –
And how the chair he sat in, and the room,
Began to look, when he had failed to come.
But as she better knew the cause than he,   320
She seemed to have the more necessity
For struggling hard, and rousing all her pride;
And so she did at first; she even tried
To feel a sort of anger at his care;
But these extremes brought but a kind despair;
And then she only spoke more sweetly to him,
And found her failing eyes give looks that melted through him.

Giovanni too, who felt relieved indeed
To see another to his place succeed,
Or rather filling up some trifling hours,   330
Better spent elsewhere, and beneath his powers,
Left the new tie to strengthen day by day,
Talked less and less, and longer kept away,
Secure in his self-love and sense of right,
That he was welcome most, come when he might.
And doubtless, they, in their still finer sense,
With added care repaid this confidence,
Turning their thoughts from his abuse of it,
To what on their own parts was graceful and was fit.

37

And now, ye gentle pair, – now think awhile,   340
Now, while ye still can think, and still can smile;
Now, while your generous hearts have not been grieved
Perhaps with something not to be retrieved,
And ye have still, within, the power of gladness,
From self-resentment free, and retrospective madness!

So did they think; – but partly from delay
Partly from fancied ignorance of the way,
And most from feeling the bare contemplation
Give them fresh need of mutual consolation.
They scarcely tried to see each other less,   350
And did but meet with deeper tenderness,
Living, from day to day, as they were used,
Only with graver thoughts, and smiles reduced,
And sighs more frequent, which, when one would heave,
The other longed to start up and receive.
For whether some suspicion now had crossed
Giovanni's mind, or whether he had lost
More of his temper lately, he would treat
His wife with petty scorns, and starts of heat,
And, to his own omissions proudly blind,   360
O'erlook the pains she took to make him kind,
And yet be angry, if he thought them less;
He found reproaches in her meek distress,
Forcing her silent tears, and then resenting,
Then almost angrier grown from half repenting,
And, hinting at the last, that some there were
Better perhaps than he, and tastefuller,
And these, for what he knew, – he little cared, –
Might please her, and be pleased, though he despaired.
Then would he quit the room, and half disdain   370
Himself for being in so harsh a strain,
And venting thus his temper on a woman;
Yet not the more for that changed he in common,
Or took more pains to please her, and be near: –

What! should he truckle to a woman's tear?

At times like these the princess tried to shun
The face of Paulo as too kind a one;
And shutting up her tears with resolute sigh,
Would walk into the air, and see the sky,
And feel about her all the garden green,   380
And hear the birds that shot the covert boughs between.

A noble range it was, of many a rood,
Walled round with trees, and ending in a wood:
Indeed the whole was leafy; and it had
A winding stream about it, clear and glad,
That danced from shade to shade, and on its way
Seemed smiling with delight to feel the day.
There was the pouting rose, both red and white,
The flamy heart's-ease, flushed with purple light,
Blush-hiding strawberry, sunny-coloured box,   390
Hyacinth, handsome with his clustering locks,
The lady lily, looking gently down,
Pure lavender, to lay in bridal gown,
The daisy, lovely on both sides, – in short,
All the sweet cups to which the bees resort,
With plots of grass, and perfumed walks between
Of citron, honeysuckle and jessamine,
With orange, whose warm leaves so finely suit,
And look as if they'd shade a golden fruit;
And midst the flowers, turfed round beneath a shade   400
Of circling pines, a babbling fountain played,
And 'twixt their shafts you saw the water bright,
Which through the darksome tops glimmered with showering
    light.
So now you walked beside an odorous bed
Of gorgeous hues, white, azure, golden, red;
And now turned off into a leafy walk,
Close and continuous, fit for lovers' talk;

And now pursued the stream, and as you trod
Onward and onward o'er the velvet sod,
Felt on your face an air, watery and sweet,   410
And a new sense in your soft-lighting feet;
And then perhaps you entered upon shades,
Pillowed with dells and uplands 'twixt the glades,
Through which the distant palace, now and then,
Looked lordly forth with many-windowed ken;
A land of trees, which reaching round about,
In shady blessing stretched their old arms out,
With spots of sunny opening, and with nooks,
To lie and read in, sloping into brooks,
Where at her drink you startled the slim deer,   420
Retreating lightly with a lovely fear.
And all about, the birds kept leafy house,
And sung and sparkled in and out the boughs;
And all about, a lovely sky of blue
Clearly was felt, or down the leaves laughed through.
And here and there, in every part, were seats,
Some in the open walks, some in retreats;
With bowering leaves o'erhead, to which the eye
Looked up half sweetly and half awfully, –
Places of nesting green, for poets made,   430
Where when the sunshine struck a yellow shade,
The slender trunks, to inward peeping sight
Thronged in dark pillars up the gold green light.

But 'twixt the wood and flowery walks, halfway,
And formed of both, the loveliest portion lay,
A spot, that struck you like enchanted ground: –
It was a shallow dell, set in a mound
Of sloping shrubs, that mounted by degrees,
The birch and poplar mixed with heavier trees;
From under which, sent through a marble spout,   440
Betwixt the dark wet green, a rill gushed out,
Whose low sweet talking seemed as if it said

Something eternal to that happy shade:
The ground within was lawn, with plots of flowers
Heaped towards the centre, and with citron bowers;
And in the midst of all, clustered about
With bay and myrtle, and just gleaming out,
Lurked a pavilion, – a delicious sight,
Small, marble, well-proportioned, mellowy white
With yellow vine-leaves sprinkled, – but no more, –   450
And a young orange either side the door.
The door was to the wood, forward, and square,
The rest was domed at top, and circular;
And through the dome the only light came in,
Tinged, as it entered, with the vine-leaves thin.

It was a beauteous piece of ancient skill,
Spared from the rage of war, and perfect still;
By most supposed the work of fairy hands,
Famed for luxurious taste, and choice of lands, –
Alcina, or Morgana, – who from fights   460
And errant fame inveigled amorous knights,
And lived with them in a long round of blisses,
Feasts, concerts, baths, and bower-enshaded kisses.
But 'twas a temple, as its scripture told,
Built to the Nymphs that haunted there of old;
For o'er the door was carved a sacrifice
By girls and shepherds brought, with reverent eyes,
Of sylvan drinks and foods, simple and sweet,
And goats with struggling horns and planted feet:
And on a line with this ran round about   470
A like relief, touched exquisitely out,
That shewed, in various scenes, the nymphs themselves;
Some by the water side on bowery shelves
Leaning at will, – some in the water sporting
With sides half swelling forth, and looks of courting, –
Some in a flowery dell, hearing a swain
Play on his pipe, till the hills ring again, –

41

Some tying up their long moist hair, – some sleeping
Under the trees, with fauns and satyrs peeping, –
Or, sidelong-eyed, pretending not to see   480
The latter in the brakes come creepingly,
While their forgotten urns, lying about
In the green herbage, let the water out.
Never, be sure, before or since was seen
A summer-house so fine in such a nest of green.

All the green garden, flower-bed, shade, and plot,
Francesca loved, but most of all this spot.
Whenever she walked forth, wherever went
About the grounds, to this at last she bent:
Here she had brought a lute and a few books;   490
Here would she lie for hours, with grateful looks,
Thanking at heart the sunshine and the leaves,
The summer rain-drops counting from the eaves,
And all that promising, calm smile we see
In nature's face, when we look patiently.
Then would she think of heaven; and you might hear
Sometimes, when every thing was hushed and clear,
Her gentle voice from out those shades emerging,
Singing the evening anthem to the Virgin.
The gardeners and the rest, who served the place,   500
And blest whenever they beheld her face,
Knelt when they heard it, bowing and uncovered,
And felt as if in air some sainted beauty hovered.

One day, – 'twas on a summer afternoon,
When airs and gurgling brooks are best in tune,
And grasshoppers are loud, and day-work done,
And shades have heavy outlines in the sun, –
The princess came to her accustomed bower
To get her, if she could, a soothing hour,
Trying, as she was used, to leave her cares   510
Without, and slumberously enjoy the airs,

And the low-talking leaves, and that cool light
The vines let in, and all that hushing sight
Of closing wood seen through the opening door,
And distant plash of waters tumbling o'er,
And smell of citron blooms, and fifty luxuries more.

She tried, as usual, for the trial's sake,
For even that diminished her heart-ache;
And never yet, how ill soe'er at ease,
Came she for nothing 'midst the flowers and trees.   520
Yet somehow or another, on that day,
She seemed to feel too lightly borne away, –
Too much relieved, – too much inclined to draw
A careless joy from every thing she saw,
And looking round her with a new-born eye,
As if some tree of knowledge had been nigh,
To taste of nature, primitive and free,
And bask at ease in her heart's liberty.

Painfully clear those rising thoughts appeared,
With something dark at bottom that she feared;   530
And snatching from the fields her thoughtful look,
She reached o'er-head, and took her down a book,
And fell to reading with as fixed an air,
As though she had been wrapt since morning there.

'Twas Launcelot of the Lake, a bright romance,
That like a trumpet, made young pulses dance,
Yet had a softer note that shook still more; –
She had begun it but the day before,
And read with a full heart, half sweet, half sad,
How old King Ban was spoiled of all he had   540
But one fair castle: how one summer's day
With his fair queen and child he went away
To ask the great King Arthur for assistance;
How reaching by himself a hill at distance

43

He turned to give his castle a last look,
And saw its far white face: and how a smoke,
As he was looking, burst in volumes forth,
And good King Ban saw all that he was worth,
And his fair castle, burning to the ground,
So that his wearied pulse felt over-wound, 550
And he lay down, and said a prayer apart
For those he loved, and broke his poor old heart.
Then read she of the queen with her young child,
How she came up, and nearly had gone wild,
And how in journeying on in her despair,
She reached a lake and met a lady there,
Who pities her, and took the baby sweet
Into her arms, when lo, with closing feet
She sprang up all at once, like bird from brake,
And vanished with him underneath the lake. 560
The mother's feelings we as well may pass: –
The fairy of the place that lady was,
And Launcelot (so the boy was called) became
Her inmate, till in search of knightly fame
He went to Arthur's court, and played his part
So rarely, and displayed so frank a heart,
That what with all his charms of look and limb,
The Queen Geneura fell in love with him: –
And here, with growing interest in her reading,
The princess, doubly fixed, was now proceeding. 570

Ready she sat with one hand to turn o'er
The leaf, to which her thoughts ran on before,
The other propping her white brow, and throwing
Its ringlets out, under the skylight glowing.
So sat she fixed; and so observed was she
Of one, who at the door stood tenderly, –
Paulo, – who from a window seeing her
Go straight across the lawn, and guessing where,
Had thought she was in tears, and found, that day,

His usual efforts vain to keep away.   580
'May I come in?' said he: – it made her start, –
That smiling voice; – she coloured, pressed her heart
A moment, as for breath, and then with free
And usual tone said, 'O yes, – certainly.'
There's apt to be, at conscious times like these,
An affectation of a bright-eyed ease,
An air of something quite serene and sure,
As if to seem so, was to be, secure:
With this the lovers met, with this they spoke,
With this they sat down to the self-same book,   590
And Paulo, by degrees, gently embraced
With one permitted arm her lovely waist;
And both their cheeks, like peaches on a tree,
Leaned with a touch together, thrillingly;
And o'er the book they hung, and nothing said,
And every lingering page grew longer as they read.

As thus they sat, and felt with leaps of heart
Their colour change, they came upon the part
Where fond Geneura, with her flame long nurst,
Smiled upon Launcelot when he kissed her first: –   600
That touch, at last, through every fibre slid;
And Paulo turned, scarce knowing what he did,
Only he felt he could no more dissemble,
And kissed her, mouth to mouth, all in a tremble.
Sad were those hearts, and sweet was that long kiss:
Sacred be love from sight, whate'er it is.
The world was all forgot, the struggle o'er.
Desperate the joy. – That day they read no more.[2]

                                   1816

                                    45

To Hampstead

As one who after long and far-spent years
  Comes on his mistress in an hour of sleep,
  And half-surprised that he can silence keep,
Stands smiling o'er her through a flash of tears,
To see how sweet and self-same she appears;
  Till at his touch, with little moving creep
  Of joy, she wakes from out her calmness deep,
And then his heart finds voice, and dances round her ears: –

So I, first coming on my haunts again,
  In pause and stillness of the early prime,
  Stood thinking of the past and present time,
With earnest eyesight, scarcely crossed with pain;
  Till the fresh moving leaves, and startling birds,
  Loosened my long-suspended breath in words.

1815

Description of Hampstead

A steeple issuing from a leafy rise,
  With farmy fields in front, and sloping green,
  Dear Hampstead, is thy southern face serene,
Silently smiling on approaching eyes.
Within, thine ever-shifting looks surprise, –
  Streets, hills, and dells, trees overhead now seen,
  Now down below, with smoking roofs between, –

A village, revelling in varieties.
The northward what a range, – with heath and pond,
  Nature's own ground; woods that let mansions through,
And cottaged vales with pillowy fields beyond,

46

And clump of darkening pines, and prospects blue,
And that clear path through all, where daily meet
Cool cheeks, and brilliant eyes, and morn-elastic feet.

1815

To the Grasshopper and the Cricket

Green little vaulter in the sunny grass,
    Catching your heart up at the feel of June,
    Sole voice that's heard amidst the lazy noon,
When ev'n the bees lag at the summoning brass; –
And you, warm little housekeeper, who class
    With those who think the candles come too soon,
    Loving the fire, and with your tricksome tune
Nick the glad silent moments as they pass; –

Oh sweet and tiny cousins, that belong,
    One to the fields, the other to the hearth,
Both have your sunshine; both, though small, are strong
    At your clear hearts; and both were sent on earth
To sing in thoughtful ears this natural song –
    In doors and out, – summer and winter, – Mirth.

1817

On a Lock of Milton's Hair

It lies before me there, and my own breath
    Stirs its thin outer threads, as though beside
    The living head I stood in honoured pride,
Talking of lovely things that conquer death.

47

Perhaps he pressed it once, or underneath
  Ran his fine fingers, when he leant, blank-eyed,
  And saw, in fancy, Adam and his bride
With their heaped locks, or his own Delphic wreath.

There seems a love in hair, though it be dead.
It is the gentlest, yet the strongest thread
  Of our frail plant, – a blossom from the tree
Surviving the proud trunk; – as if it said,
  Patience and Gentleness is Power. In me
  Behold affectionate eternity.

1818

The Nile

It flows through old hushed Egypt and its sands,
  Like some grave mighty thought threading a dream,
  And times and things, as in that vision, seem
Keeping along it their eternal stands, –
Caves, pillars, pyramids, the shepherd bands
  That roamed through the young world, the glory extreme
  Of high Sesostris, and that southern beam,
The laughing queen that caught the world's great hands.

Then comes a mightier silence, stern and strong,
As of a world left empty of its throng,
  And the void weighs on us; and then we wake,
And hear the fruitful stream lapsing along
  Twixt villages, and think how we shall take
  Our own calm journey on for human sake.

1818

To T.L.H.
Six years old, during a sickness

Sleep breathes at last from out thee,
   My little, patient Boy;
And balmy rest about thee
   Smooths off the day's annoy.
     I sit me down, and think
     Of all thy winning ways;
Yet almost wish, with sudden shrink,
   That I had less to praise.

Thy sidelong pillowed meekness,
   Thy thanks to all that aid,
Thy heart, in pain and weakness,
   Of fancied faults afraid;
     The little trembling hand
     That wipes thy quiet tears,
These, these are things that may demand
   Dread memories for years.

Sorrows I've had, severe ones,
   I will not think of now;
And calmly, midst my dear ones,
   Have wasted with dry brow;
     But when thy fingers press
     And pat my stooping head,
I cannot bear the gentleness, –
   The tears are in their bed.

Ah, first-born of thy mother,
   When life and hope were new,
Kind playmate of thy brother,
   Thy sister, father too;
     My light, where'er I go,
     My bird, when prison-bound,

49

My hand in hand companion, – no,
   My prayers shall hold thee round.

To say 'He has departed' –
   'His voice' – 'his face' – 'is gone';
To feel impatient-hearted,
   Yet feel we must bear on;
      Ah, I could not endure
      To whisper of such woe,
Unless I felt this sleep ensure
   That it will not be so.

   Yes, still he's fixed, and sleeping!
      This silence too the while –
   Its very hush and creeping
      Seem whispering us a smile: –
         Something divine and dim
         Seems going by one's ear,
Like parting wings of Cherubim,
   Who say, 'We've finished here.'
                                    1816

To a Lady who wished to see him
from the French of Clement Marot

She loved me, as she read my books,
   And wished to see my face;
Grey was my beard, and dark my looks;
   They lost me not her grace.

O gentle heart, O noble brow,
   Full rightly didst thou see;
For this poor lady, failing now,
   Is but my jail, not me.

Those eyes of thine found hope, and youth,
　　And vigour in my page;
And saw me better there in truth,
　　Than through the mists of age.

1830

Song
from the French of Clement Marot

I'm belov'd of one so fair,
　　Heaven beholds no beauty like her;
Envious eyes, and pens, beware;
　　Not a glance must dare to strike her.

Could the boy with blinded eyes
　　But unblind them to behold her;
He would own the sweet surprise
　　And with loving arms enfold her.

1830

From *Captain Sword and Captain Pen*

ADVERTISEMENT, 1835

This Poem is the result of a sense of duty, which has taken the Author from quieter studies during a public crisis. He obeys the impulse with joy, because it took the shape of verse; but with more pain, on some accounts, than he chooses to express. However, he has done what he conceived himself bound to do; and if every zealous lover of his species were to express his feelings in like manner, to the best of his ability, individual opinions, little

in themselves, would soon amount to an overwhelming authority, and hasten the day of reason and beneficience.

The measure is regular with an irregular aspect – four accents
in a verse, – like that of Christabel, or some of the poems of Sir
Walter Scott:

> Càptain Swòrd got ùp one dày –
> And the flàg full of hònour, as thòugh it could fèel –

He mentions this, not, of course, for readers in general, but for
the sake of those daily acceders to the list of the reading public,
whose knowledge of books is not yet equal to their love of them.

CANTO II
How Captain Sword won a great victory

Through fair and through foul went Captain Sword,
Pacer of highway and piercer of ford,
Steady of face in rain or sun.
He and his merry men, all as one;
Till they came to a place, where in battle-array
Stood thousands of faces firm as they,
Waiting to see which best could maintain   60
Bloody argument, lords of pain;
And down the throats of their fellow-men
Thrust the draught never drunk again.

   It was a spot of rural peace,
Ripening with the year's increase,
And singing in the sun with birds,
Like a maiden with happy words –
With happy words which she scarcely hears
In her own contented ears,
Such abundance feeleth she   70
Of all comfort carelessly,
Throwing round her, as she goes,

Sweet half-thoughts on lily and rose,
Nor guesseth what will soon arouse
All ears – that murder's in the house;
And that, in some strange wrong of brain,
Her father hath her mother slain.

   Steady! steady! The masses of men
Wheel, and fall in, and wheel again,
Softly as circles drawn with pen.   80

   Then a gaze there was, and valour, and fear,
And the jest that died in the jester's ear,
And preparation, noble to see,
Of all-accepting mortality;
Tranquil Necessity gracing Force;
And the trumpets danced with the stirring horse;
And lordly voices, here and there,
Called to war through the gentle air;
When suddenly, with its voice of doom
Spoke the cannon 'twixt glare and gloom,   90
Making wider the dreadful room:
On the faces of nations round
Fell the shadow of that sound.

   Death for death! The storm begins;
Rush the drums in a torrent of dins;
Crash the muskets, gash the swords;
Shoes grow red in a thousand fords;
Now for the flint, and the cartridge bite;
Darkly gathers the breath of the fight,
Salt to the palate, and stinging to sight;   100
Muskets are pointed they scarce know where;
No matter: Murder is cluttering there.
Reel the hollows: close up! close up!
Death feeds thick, and his food is his cup.
Down go bodies, snap burst eyes;

Trod on the ground are tender cries;
Brains are dashed against plashing ears;
Hah! no time has battle for tears;
Cursing helps better – cursing, that goes
Slipping through friends' blood, athirst for foes'.   110
What have soldiers with tears to do? –
We, who this mad-house must now go through,
This twenty-fold Bedlam, let loose with knives –
To murder, and stab, and grow liquid with lives –
Gasping, staring, treading red mud,
Till the drunkenness' self makes us steady of blood?

[Oh! shrink not thou, reader! Thy part's in it, too;
Has not thy praise made the thing they go through
Shocking to read of, but noble to do?]

No time to be 'breather of thoughtful breath'   120
Has the giver and taker of dreadful death.

See where comes the horse-tempest again,
Visible earthquake, bloody of mane!
Part are upon us, with edges of pain;
Part burst, riderless, over the plain,
Crashing their spurs, and twice slaying the slain.
See, by the living God! see those foot
Charging down hill – hot, hurried, and mute!
They loll their tongues out! Ah-hah! pell-mell!
Horses roll in a human hell;   130
Horse and man they climb one another –
Which is the beast, and which is the brother?
Mangling, stifling, stopping shrieks
With the tread of torn-out cheeks,
Drinking each other's bloody breath –
Here's the fleshiest feast of Death.
An odour, as of a slaughter-house,
The distant raven's dark eye bows.

Victory! victory! Man flies man;
Cannibal patience hath done what it can –   140
Carved, and been carved, drunk the drinkers down,
And now there is one that hath won the crown; –
One pale visage stands lord of the board –
Joy to the trumpets of Captain Sword!

His trumpets blow strength, his trumpets neigh,
They and his horse, and waft him away;
They and his foot, with a tired proud flow,
Tattered escapers and givers of woe.
Open, ye cities! Hats off! hold breath!
To see the man who has been with Death;   150
To see the man who determineth right
By the virtue-perplexing virtue of might.
Sudden before him have ceased the drums,
And lo! in the air of empire he comes.

All things present, in earth and sky,
Seem to look at his looking eye.[1]

                                                                          1835

From the *Autobiography*

The *Examiner* commenced at the time when Bonaparte was at
the height of his power. He had the Continent at his feet; and
three of his brothers were on thrones.

I thought of Bonaparte at that time as I have thought ever since;
to wit, that he was a great soldier, and little else; that he was not
a man of the highest order of intellect, much less a cosmopolite;
that he was a retrospective rather than a prospective man, ambitious
of old renown instead of new; and would advance the age as far,
and no farther, as suited his views of personal aggrandizement.

The *Examiner*, however much it differed with the military policy of Bonaparte's antagonists, or however meanly it thought of their understandings, never overrated his own, or was one of his partisans.

I now look upon war as one of the fleeting necessities of things in the course of human progress; as an evil (like most other evils) to be regarded in relation to some other evil that would have been worse without it, but always to be considered as an indication of comparative barbarism – as a necessity, the perpetuity of which is not to be assumed – or as a half-reasoning mode of adjustment, whether of disputes or of populations, which mankind, on arriving at years of discretion, and coming to a better understanding with one another, may, and must of necessity, do away. It would be as ridiculous to associate the idea of war with an earth covered with railroads and commerce, as a fight between Holborn and the Strand, or between people met in a drawing-room. Wars, like all other evils, have not been without their good. They have pioneered human intercourse; have thus prepared even for their own eventual abolition; and their follies, losses, and horrors have been made the best of by adornments and music, and consoled by the exhibition of many noble qualities. There is no evil unmixed with, or unproductive of, good. It could not, in the nature of things, exist. Antagonism itself prevents it. But nature incites us to the diminution of evil; and while it is pious to make the best of what is inevitable, it is no less so to obey the impulse which she had given us towards thinking and making it otherwise.

With respect to the charge of republicanism against the *Examiner*, it was as ridiculous as the rest. Both Napoleon and the Allies did, indeed, so conduct themselves on the high roads of empire and royalty, and the British sceptre was at the same time so unfortunately wielded, that kings and princes were often treated with less respect in our pages than we desired. But we generally felt, and often expressed, a wish to treat them otherwise. The *Examiner* was always quoting against them the Alfreds and Antoninuses of old. The 'Constitution', with its King, Lords, and Commons, was its incessant watchword. The greatest political change which it desired was Reform in Parliament; and it helped to obtain it, because it was in earnest. As to republics, the United States, notwithstanding our family relationship, were no favourites with us, owing to what appeared to us to be an absorption in the love of money, and to their *then* want of the imaginative and ornamental; and the excesses of the French Revolution we held in abhorrence.

1859

The Fish, the Man, and the Spirit

TO A FISH

You strange, astonished-looking, angle-faced,
   Dreary-mouthed, gaping wretches of the sea,
   Gulping salt-water everlastingly,
Cold-blooded, though with red your blood be graced,
And mute, though dwellers in the roaring waste;
   And you, all shapes beside, that fishy be, –
   Some round, some flat, some long, all devilry,
Legless, unloving, infamously chaste: –

O scaly, slippery, wet, swift, staring wights,
   What is't ye do? What life lead? eh, dull goggles?
How do ye vary your vile days and nights?
   How pass your Sundays? Are ye still but joggles
In ceaseless wash? Still nought but gapes, and bites,
   And drinks, and stares, diversified with boggles?

A FISH ANSWERS

Amazing monster! that, for aught I know,
   With the first sight of thee didst make our race
   For ever stare! O flat and shocking face,
Grimly divided from the breast below!

Thou that on dry land horribly dost go
　　With a split body and most ridiculous pace,
　　Prong after prong, disgracer of all grace,
Long-useless-finned, haired, upright, unwet, slow!

O breather of unbreathable, sword-sharp air,
　　How canst exist? How bear thyself, thou dry
And dreary sloth? What particle canst share
　　Of the only blessed life, the watery?
I sometimes see of ye an actual *pair*
　　Go by! linked fin by fin! most odiously.

THE FISH TURNS INTO A MAN, AND THEN INTO A SPIRIT, AND AGAIN SPEAKS

Indulge thy smiling scorn, if smiling still,
　　O man! and loathe, but with a sort of love;
　　For difference must its use by difference prove,
And, in sweet clang, the spheres with music fill.
One of the spirits am I, that at his will
　　Live in whate'er has life – fish, eagle, dove –
　　No hate, no pride, beneath nought, nor above,
A visitor of the rounds of God's sweet skill.

Man's life is warm, glad, sad, 'twixt loves and graves,
　　Boundless in hope, honoured with pangs austere,
Heaven-gazing; and his angel-wings he craves: –
　　The fish is swift, small-needing, vague yet clear,
A cold, sweet, silver life, wrapped in round waves,
　　Quickened with touches of transporting fear.

1836

Abou Ben Adhem

Abou Ben Adhem (may his tribe increase!)
Awoke one night from a deep dream of peace,
And saw, within the moonlight in his room,
Making it rich, and like a lily in bloom,
An angel writing in a book of gold: –
Exceeding peace had made Ben Adhem bold,
And to the presence in the room he said,
'What writest thou?' – The vision raised its head,
And with a look made of all sweet accord,
Answered, 'The names of those who love the Lord.'
'And is mine one?' said Abou. 'Nay, not so,'
Replied the angel. Abou spoke more low,
But cheerly still; and said, 'I pray thee then,
Write me as one that loves his fellow-men.'

   The angel wrote, and vanished. The next night
It came again with a great wakening light,
And showed the names whom love of God had blessed,
And lo! Ben Adhem's name led all the rest.

1838

Rondeau[1]

Jenny kissed me when we met,
   Jumping from the chair she sat in;
Time, you thief, who love to get
   Sweets into your list, put that in:
Say I'm weary, say I'm sad,
   Say that health and wealth have missed me,
Say I'm growing old, but add,
   Jenny kissed me.

1838

From *A Rustic Walk and Dinner*

PART I: THE WALK

How fine to walk to dinner, not too far,
Through a green country, on a summer's day,
The dinner at an inn, the time our own,
The roads not dusty, yet the fields not wet,
The grass *lie-down-upónable*. – Avaunt,
Critics, or come with us, and learn the right
Of coining words in the quick mint of joy.

Pleasant is horseback, – the light strenuous dance
Upon the saddle, talking as we go,
With voices lifted jovial, 'midst the churme   10
Of leathers and clutched earth, that on the ear
Of sitters within doors lies far away.
Pleasant is rolling onward in a coach,
All ease and cushion; more especially
If you see some one's head bob up and down,
Poor devil! by the side of it, in run
Emulous and tired (so cruel-comfortable
Does luxury make us). Pleasant, also, boating,
Provided you can pull – and are not bound
To pull too much, and look angry and hot,   20
Pretending you are easy. Roundly go
The wrists, and cluck the rullocks, and the oar
Chucks from its spoon the water with a grace.
So boaters feather. – Pleasant is a sail,
Spanking and spitting through some roughening frith,
When the white foam grows whiter for a cloud,
And sunshine's out at sea; – Or pleasanter,
Methinks, 'for a continuance', between banks
Of inland green; when, gliding, the sail swells
Mild as your lady's bosom; and the swan   30
Stirs not from where it sits fastidious,
Breasting the pouting of its own regard.

But walking's freest. Riding, you must keep
To roads; coaching, still more so; and your boat
Must be got home. In walking, you command
Time, place, caprice; may go on, or return,
Lie down, expatiate, wander; laugh at gates,
That poze the loftiest-minded fox-hunter;
Hills animate, brooks lull, woods welcome you,
Like lovers' whispers; you may go within,   40
Into the secret'st shade, and there climb banks
And bowers of rooty and weedy luxury,
Knee-deep in flowers, upborne by nutty boughs,
Into a paradise of sunny shade,
And sit, and read your book, beside the birds

    And lo! we do so; we, the reader and I,
Who tow'rds our inn thus far have come from town,
Now loose, now arm-linked, – first by suburb-garden,
Half-box, half pavement, – and the long brick wall
Vociferous with 'Warren', – and the turnpike,   50
With pocket-aproned man, jingling his cash, –
And the high road, with its dry ditch dock-leaved, –
And ever-met horseman and wagoner
Slouching, and jockey-capped postilion trim,
Interminable of dance on horse's back, –
And then by field-paths, and more flowery ditch
White-starred, and red, and azure, – and through all
Those heaps of buttercups, that smear the land
With splendour, nearly extinguishing the daisies, –
And hill, and dale, and stile on which we sat   60
Cooling our brows under the airy trees,
And heard the brook low down, and found that hunk
Of bread so exquisite, to the very crumbs
That shared a pocket-corner with its halfpence. –
(O Shelley! 'twas a bond 'twixt thee and me,
That power to eat the sweet crust out of doors!
You laughed with loving eyes, wrinkled with mirth,

And cried, high breathing, 'What! can you do *that*?
I thought that no one dared a thing so strange
And primitive, but myself.' – And so we loved   70
Ever the more, and found our love increase
Most by such simple abidings with boy-wisdom.)....

1842

To Charles Dickens

As when a friend (himself in music's list)
Stands by some rare, full-handed organist,
And glorying as he sees the master roll
The surging sweets through all their depths of soul,
Cannot, encouraged by his smile, forbear
With his own hand to join them here and there;
And so, if little, yet add something more
To the sound's volume and the golden roar;

So I, dear friend, Charles Dickens, though thy hand
Needs but itself, to charm from land to land,
Make bold to join in summoning men's ears
To this thy new-found music of our spheres,
In hopes that by thy Household Words and thee
The world may haste to days of harmony.

1860

On the Death of His Son Vincent[1]

Waking at morn, with the accustomed sigh
For what no more could ever bring me more,
And again sighing, while collecting strength
To meet the pangs that waited me, like one
Whose sleep the rack hath watched: I tried to feel
How good for me had been strange griefs of old,
That for long days, months, years, inured my wits
To bear the dreadful burden of one thought.
One thought with woeful need turned many ways,
Which, shunned at first, and scaring me, as wounds
Thrusting in wound, became, oh! almost clasped
And blest, as saviours from the one dire pang
That mocked the will to move it.

1862

An Answer to the Question
What is Poetry?
including
Remarks on Versification

Poetry, strictly and artistically so called, that is to say, considered not merely as poetic feeling, which is more or less shared by all the world, but as the operation of that feeling, such as we see it in the poet's book, is the utterance of a passion for truth, beauty, and power, embodying and illustrating its conceptions by imagination and fancy, and modulating its language on the principle of variety in uniformity. Its means are whatever the universe contains; and its ends, pleasure and exaltation. Poetry stands between nature and convention, keeping alive among us the enjoyment of the external and the spiritual world: it has constituted the most enduring fame of nations; and, next to Love and Beauty, which are its parents, is the greatest proof to man of the pleasure to be found in all things, and of the probable riches of infinitude.

Poetry is a passion,* because it seeks the deepest impressions; and because it must undergo, in order to convey them.

It is a passion for truth, because without truth the impression would be false or defective.

It is a passion for beauty, because its office is to exalt and refine by means of pleasure, and because beauty is nothing but the loveliest form of pleasure.

It is a passion for power, because power is impression triumphant, whether over the poet, as desired by himself, or over the reader, as affected by the poet.

It embodies and illustrates its impressions by imagination, or images of the objects of which it treats, and other images brought in to throw light on those objects, in order that it may enjoy and impart the feeling of their truth in its utmost conviction and affluence.

* *Passio*, suffering in a good sense, – ardent subjection of oneself to emotion.

It illustrates them by fancy, which is a lighter play of imagination, or the feeling of analogy coming short of seriousness, in order that it may laugh with what it loves, and show how it can decorate it with fairy ornament.

It modulates what it utters, because in running the whole round of beauty it must needs include beauty of sound; and because, in the height of its enjoyment, it must show the perfection of its triumph, and make difficulty itself become part of its facility and joy.

And lastly, Poetry shapes this modulation into uniformity for its outline, and variety for its parts, because it thus realizes the last idea of beauty itself, which includes the charm of diversity within the flowing round of habit and ease.

Poetry is imaginative passion. The quickest and subtlest test of the possession of its essence is in expression; the variety of things to be expressed shows the amount of its resources; and the continuity of the song completes the evidence of its strength and greatness. He who has thought, feeling, expression, imagination, action, character, and continuity, all in the largest amount and highest degree, is the greatest poet. . . .

There are different kinds and degrees of imagination, some of them necessary to the formation of every true poet, and all of them possessed by the greatest. Perhaps they may be enumerated as follows: – First, that which presents to the mind any object or circumstance in everyday life; as when we imagine a man holding a sword, or looking out of a window; – Second, that which presents real, but not everyday circumstances; as King Alfred tending the loaves, or Sir Philip Sidney giving up the water to the dying soldier; – Third, that which combines character and events directly imitated from real life, with imitative realities of its own invention; as the probable parts of the histories of *Priam* and *Macbeth*, or what may be called natural fiction as distinguished from supernatural; – Fourth, that which conjures up things and events not to be found in nature; as Homer's gods, and Shakspeare's witches, enchanted horses and spears, Ariosto's hippogriff, etc.; – Fifth, that which, in order to illustrate or aggravate one image, introduces another: sometimes in simile, as when Homer compares Apollo descending in his wrath at noon-day to the coming of night-time; sometimes in metaphor, or simile comprised in a word, as in Milton's 'motes that *people* the sunbeams'; sometimes in concentrating into a word the main history of any person or thing, past or even future, as in the 'starry Galileo' of Byron, and that ghastly foregone conclusion of the epithet 'murdered' applied to the yet living victim in Keats's story from Boccaccio, –

> So the two brothers and their *murder'd* man
> Rode towards fair Florence; –

sometimes in the attribution of a certain representative quality which makes one circumstance stand for others; as in Milton's grey-fly winding its '*sultry* horn', which epithet contains the heat of a summer's day; – Sixth, that which reverses this process, and makes a variety of circumstances take colour from one, like nature seen with jaundiced or glad eyes, or under the influence of storm or sunshine; as when in Lycidas, or the Greek pastoral poets, the flowers and the flocks are made to sympathize with a man's death; or, in the Italian poet, the river flowing by the sleeping Angelica seems talking of love –

> Parea che l' erba le fiorisse intorno,
> E d' amor ragionasse quella riva! –
> – *Orlando Innamorato*, canto iii[1]

or in the voluptuous homage paid to the sleeping Imogen by the very light in the chamber and the reaction of her own beauty upon itself; or in the 'witch element' of the tragedy of *Macbeth* and the May-day night of *Faust*; – Seventh, and last, that which by a single expression, apparently of the vaguest kind, not only meets but surpasses in its effect the extremest force of the most particular description; as in that exquisite passage of Coleridge's *Christabel*, where the unsuspecting object of the witch's malignity is bidden to go to bed: –

66

> Quoth Christabel, So let it be:
> And as the lady bade, did she.
> Her gentle limbs did she undress,
> *And lay down in her loveliness*; –

a perfect verse surely, both for feeling and music. The very smoothness and gentleness of the limbs is in the series of letter *l*'s.

I am aware of nothing of the kind surpassing that most lovely inclusion of physical beauty in moral, neither can I call to mind any instances of the imagination that turns accompaniments into accessories, superior to those I have alluded to. Of the class of comparison, one of the most touching (many a tear must it have drawn from parents and lovers) is in a stanza which has been copied into the *Friar of Orders Grey*, out of Beaumont and Fletcher: –

> Weep no more, lady, weep no more,
> Thy sorrow is in vain;
> *For violets pluck'd the sweetest showers*
> *Will ne'er make grow again.*

And Shakspeare and Milton abound in the very grandest; such as Antony's likening his changing fortunes to the cloud-rack; Lear's appeal to the old age of the heavens; Satan's appearance in the horizon, like a fleet 'hanging in the clouds'; and the comparisons of him with the comet and the eclipse. Nor unworthy of this glorious company, for its extraordinary combination of delicacy and vastness, is that enchanting one of Shelley's in the *Adonais*: –

> Life, like a dome of many-coloured glass,
> Stains the white radiance of eternity.

I multiply these particulars in order to impress upon the reader's mind the great importance of imagination in all its phases as a constituent part of the highest poetic faculty. . . .

With regard to the principle of Variety in Uniformity by which verse ought to be modulated, and one-ness of impression diversely produced, it has been contended by some, that Poetry need not be written in verse at all; that prose is as good a medium, provided poetry be conveyed through it; and that to think otherwise is to confound letter with spirit, or form with essence. But the opinion is a prosaical mistake. Fitness and unfitness for *song*, or metrical excitement, just make all the difference between a poetical and prosaical subject; and the reason why verse is necessary to the form of poetry is, that the perfection of poetical spirit demands it; – that the circle of its enthusiasm, beauty, and power, is incomplete without it. I do not mean to say that a poet can never show himself a poet in prose; but that, being one, his desire and necessity will be to write in verse; and that, if he were unable to do so, he would not, and could not, deserve his title. Verse to the true poet is no clog. It is idly called a trammel and a difficulty. It is a help. It springs from the same enthusiasm as the rest of his impulses, and is necessary to their satisfaction and effect. Verse is no more a clog than the condition of rushing upward is a clog to fire, or than the roundness and order of the globe we live on is a clog to the freedom and variety that abound within its sphere. Verse is no denominator over the poet, except inasmuch as the bond is reciprocal, and the poet dominates over the verse. They are lovers, playfully challenging each other's rule, and delighted equally to rule and to obey. Verse is the final proof to the poet that his mastery over his art is complete. It is the shutting up of his powers in '*measureful* content'; the answer of form to his spirit; of strength and ease to his guidance. It is the willing action, the proud and fiery happiness, of the winged steed on whose back he has vaulted, 'To witch the world with wondrous horsemanship'. Verse, in short, is that finishing, and rounding, and 'tuneful planetting' of the poet's creations, which is produced of necessity by the smooth tendencies of their energy or inward working, and the harmonious dance into which they are attracted round the orb of the beautiful. Poetry, in its complete sympathy with beauty, must, of necessity, leave no sense of the beautiful, and no power over its forms, unmanifested; and verse flows as inevitably from this condition of its integrity, as other laws of proportion do from any other kind of embodiment of beauty (say that of the human figure), however free and various the movements may be that play within their limits. . . .

What the poet has to cultivate above all things is love and truth; – what he has to avoid, like poison, is the fleeting and the false. He will get no good by proposing to be 'in earnest at the moment'. His earnestness must be innate and habitual; born with him, and felt to be his most precious inheritance. 'I expect neither profit nor general fame by my writings,' says Coleridge, in the Preface to his Poems; 'and I consider myself as having been amply repaid without either. Poetry has been to me, its *"own exceeding great reward"*; it has soothed my afflictions; it has multiplied and refined my enjoyments; it has endeared solitude; and it has given me the habit of wishing to discover the good and the beautiful in all that meets and surrounds me.'

'Poetry,' says Shelley, 'lifts the veil from the hidden beauty of the world, *and makes familiar objects be as if they were not familiar.* It reproduces all that it represents; and the impersonations clothed in its Elysian light stand thenceforward in the minds of those who have once contemplated them, as memorials of that gentle and exalted content which extends itself over all thoughts and actions with which it co-exists. The great secret of morals is love, or a going out of our own nature, and an identification of ourselves with the beautiful which exists in thought, action, or person, not our own. A man, to be greatly good, must imagine intensely and comprehensively; he must put himself in the place of another, and of many others: the pains and pleasures of his own species must become his own. The great instrument of moral good is imagination; and poetry administers to the effect by acting upon the cause.' – *Essays and Letters*, vol.I, p.16.

I would not willingly say anything after perorations like these; but as treatises on poetry may chance to have auditors who think themselves called upon to vindicate the superiority of what is termed useful knowledge, it may be as well to add, that if the poet may be allowed to pique himself on any one thing more than another, compared with those who undervalue him, it is on that power of undervaluing nobody, and no attainments different from his own, which is given him by the very faculty of imagination they despise. The greater includes the less. They do not see that their inability to comprehend him argues the smaller capacity. No man recognizes the worth of utility more than the poet: he only desires that the meaning of the term may not come short of its greatness, and exclude the noblest necessities of his fellow-creatures. He is quite as much pleased, for instance, with the facilities for rapid conveyance afforded him by the railroad, as the dullest confiner of its advantages to that single idea, or as the greatest two-idea'd man who varies that single idea with hugging himself on his 'buttons' or his good dinner. But he sees also the beauty of the country through which he passes, of the towns, of the heavens, of the steam-engine itself, thundering and fuming along like a magic horse, of the affections that are carrying, perhaps, half the passengers on their journey, nay, of those of the great two-idea'd man; and, beyond all this, he discerns the incalculable amount of good, and knowledge, and refinement, and mutual consideration, which this wonderful invention is fitted to circulate over the globe, perhaps to the displacement of war itself, and certainly to the diffusion of millions of enjoyments. . . .

'And a button-maker, after all, invented it!' cries our friend.

Pardon me – it was a nobleman. A button-maker may be a very excellent, and a very poetical man too, and yet not have been the first man visited by a sense of the gigantic powers of the combination of water and fire. It was a nobleman who first thought of this most poetical bit of science. It was a nobleman who first thought of it, – a captain who first tried it, – and a button-maker who perfected it. And he who put the nobleman on such thoughts was the great philosopher, Bacon, who said that poetry had 'something divine in it', and was necessary to the satisfaction of the human mind.

1844

From the Preface to *Stories in Verse*

Containing Remarks on the Father of English Narrative Poetry; on the Ill-understood Nature of Heroic Verse; on the Necessity, Equally Ill-understood, of the Musical Element in Poetry to Poetry in General; and on the Absurdity of Confining the Name of Poetry to Any One Species of It in Particular

As this book, in issuing from the house of Messrs Routledge acquires a special chance of coming under the cognizance of travellers by the railway, I have pleased myself with fancying that it gives me a kind of new link, however remote like the rest, with my great master in the art of poetry; that is to say, with the great master of English narrative in verse, the Father of our Poetry itself, Chaucer.

Nay, it gives me two links, one general, and one particular; for as Chaucer's stories, in default of there being any printed books and travelling carriages in those days, were related by travellers to one another, and as these stories will be read, and (I hope) shown to one another, by travellers who are descendants of those travellers (see how the links thicken as we advance!), so one of Chaucer's stories concerned a wonderful Magic Horse; and now, one of the most wonderful of all such horses will be speeding my readers and me together to all parts of the kingdom, with a fire hitherto unknown to any horse whatsoever.

How would the great poet have been delighted to see the creature! – and what would he not have said of it!

I say 'creature', because though your fiery Locomotive is a creation of man's, as that of the poet was, yet as the poet's 'wondrous Horse of Brass' was formed out of ideas furnished him by Nature, so, out of elements no less furnished by Nature, and the first secrets of which are no less amazing, has been formed this wonderful Magic Horse of Iron and Steam, which, with vitals of fire, clouds literally flowing from its nostrils, and a bulk, a rushing, and a panting like that of some huge antediluvian wild beast, is now heard and seen in all parts of the country, and in most parts of civilized Europe, breaking up the old grounds of alienation,

71

and carrying with it the seeds of universal brotherhood.

Verily, something even of another, but most grating link, starts up out of that reflection upon the poet's miracle; for the hero who rode his horse of brass made war with Russia; and we Englishmen, the creators of the Horse of Iron, are warring with the despot of the same barbarous country, pitting the indignant genius of civilization against his ruffianly multitudes.

> At Sarra, in the land of Tartariè,
> There dwelt a king that warried Russiè,
> Through which there died many a doughty man.[1]

Many a doughty man, many a noble heart of captain and of common soldier, has perished in this new war against the old ignorance; an ignorance that by its sullen persistence in rejecting the kindly advice of governments brave and great enough to be peaceful, forced the very enthusiasts of peace (myself among the number) into the conviction that out of hatred and loathing of war itself, war must be made upon him.[2] If a lunatic will not put down his sword, and there is no other mode of restraining him, the sword must put down the lunatic.

May there be such a tale to tell of him as shall surpass in its results the most compensating terminations of story-books, and even the marvels of the affecting heroism with which his multitudes have been overthrown! I am not sure that the friendship which the war has occasioned between France and England is not alone sufficient to pay for it; yet war is so atrocious an evil, and those who personally and mentally suffer by it have alone such a right to the casting votes in its question, that all who sit at home by their firesides in safety and in comfort ought finally to contemplate nothing but its extinction. Gather those votes on fields of battle, on fields after the battle, in hospitals, in bereaved homes, in sorrowing and sicklied generations, and then talk of 'opinions' on the subject.

How can the man Nicholas lie in his bed, and think of the miseries, in body and in soul, which he inflicts on millions of his fellow-creatures!

But he talks of 'God!' and when such a man talks of God, the case becomes hopeless. Assassins talk so. Massacrers of Protestant and of Papist talked so. His ancestors talked so, when they slew one another; and other murderers talked so, when they slew others of the ancestors. The strangulations by which Nicholas's father and grandfather, and some think even his brother Alexander perished were justified by such talk. Will nothing teach him the peril of it? Are 'instruments in the hands of Providence' never chucked away into corners, and treated with the greatest contempt?

But I must not be forgetting story for history.

Let me take this opportunity of recommending such readers as are not yet acquainted with Chaucer to make up for their lost time. The advice is not to my benefit, but it is greatly to theirs, and loyalty to him forces me to speak. The poet's 'old English' is no difficulty, if they will but believe it. A little study would soon make them understand it as easily as that of most provincial dialects. Chaucer is the greatest narrative poet in the language; that is to say, the greatest and best teller of stories, in the understood sense of that term. He is greatest in every respect, and in the most opposite qualifications; greatest in pathos, greatest in pleasantry, greatest in character, greatest in plot, greatest even in versification, if the unsettled state of the language in his time, and the want of all native precursors in the art, be considered; for his verse is anything but the rugged and formless thing it has been supposed to be; and if Dryden surpassed him in it, not only was the superiority owing to the master's help, but there were delicate and noble turns and cadences in the old poet, which the poet of the age of Charles the Second wanted spiritually enough to appreciate....

... Chaucer's country disgraced itself for upwards of a century by considering the Father of its Poetry as nothing but an obsolete jester. Even poets thought so, in consequence of a prevailing ignorance of nine-tenths of his writing, originating in the gross tastes of the age of Charles the Second. There are passages, it is true, in Chaucer which for the sake of all parties, persons of thorough delicacy will never read twice; for they were compliances with the licence of an age in which the court itself, his sphere, was as clownish in some of its tastes as the unqualified admirers of Swift and Prior are now; and the great poet lamented that he had condescended to write them. But by far the greatest portion of his works is full of delicacies of every kind, of the noblest sentiment, of the purest, most various, and most profound entertainment.

Postponing, however, what I have to say further on the subject of Chaucer, it becomes, I am afraid, a little too obviously proper, as well as more politic, to return, in this Preface, to the book of the humblest of his followers.

I have taken occasion from this collection of my narrative poems to reprint the *Story of Rimini* according to its first size and treatment. I have done this in compliance not only with my own judgment, but with that (as far as I could ascertain it) of the majority of my readers. The refashionment of the poem was always an unwilling and I now believe was a mistaken concession to what I supposed to be the ascertained facts of the story and the better conveyance of the moral. I have since discovered that there are no ascertained facts which disallow my first conceptions of either; and it is with as much pleasure as a modest sense of the pretensions of my performance will allow, that I restore those passages relating to the sorrows of the wife, and to the fatal conflict of the brothers, which have been honoured with the tears of some of the manliest as well as tenderest eyes. . . .

When I wrote the *Story of Rimini*, which was between the years 1812 and 1815, I was studying versification in the school of Dryden. Masterly as my teacher was, I felt, without knowing it, that there was a want in him, even in versification; and the supply of this want, later in life, I found in his far greater master, Chaucer; for though Dryden's versification is noble, beautiful, and so complete of its kind that to an ear uninstructed in the metre of the old poet all comparison between the two in this respect seems out of the question, and even ludicrous, yet the measure in which Dryden wrote not only originated, but attained to a considerable degree of its beauty, in Chaucer; and the old poet's immeasurable superiority in sentiment and imagination, not only to Dryden, but to all, up to a very late period, who have written in the same form of verse, left him in possession of beauties, even in versification, which it remains for some future poet to amalgamate with Dryden's in a manner worthy of both, and so carry England's noble heroic rhythm to its pitch of perfection.

Critics, and poets too, have greatly misconceived the rank and requirements of this form of verse, who have judged it from the smoothness and monotony which it died of towards the close of the last century, and from which nothing was thought necessary for its resuscitation but an opposite unsystematic extreme. A doubt, indeed, of a very curious and hitherto unsuspected, or at least unnoticed nature, may be entertained by inquirers into the musical portion of the art of poetry (for poetry is an art as well as a gift); namely, whether, since the time of Dryden, any poets whatsoever, up to the period above alluded to (and very few indeed have done otherwise since then), thought of versification as a thing necessary to be studied at all, with the exceptions of Gray and Coleridge.

The case remains the same at present; but such assuredly was not the case either with Dryden himself, or with any of the greater poets before him, the scholarly ones in particular, such as Spenser, Milton, and their father Chaucer, who was as learned as any of them for the time in which he lived, and well acquainted with metres, French, Latin, and Italian.

Poets less reverent to their art, out of a notion that the gift, in their instance, is of itself sufficient for all its purposes (which is much as if a musician should think he could do without studying thorough-bass, or a painter without studying drawing and colours), trust to an ear which is often not good enough to do justice to the amount of gift which they really possess; and hence comes a loss, for several generations together, of the whole musical portion of poetry, to the destruction of its beauty in tone and in movement, and the peril of much good vitality in new writers. For proportions, like all other good things, hold together; and he

75

that is wanting in musical feeling where music is required, is in danger of being discordant and disproportionate in sentiment, of not perceiving the difference between thoughts worthy and unworthy of utterance. It is for this reason among others that he pours forth 'crotchets' in abundance, not in unison with his theme, and wanting in harmony with one another.

There is sometimes a kind of vague and (to the apprehensions of the unmusical) senseless melody, which in lyrical compositions, the song in particular, really constitutes, in the genuine poetical sense of the beautiful, what the scorner of it says it falsely and foolishly constitutes – namely, a good half of its merit. It answers to variety and expression of tone in a beautiful voice, and to 'air', grace, and freedom in the movements of a charming person. The Italians, in their various terms for the beautiful, have a word for it precisely answering to the first feeling one has in attempting to express it – *vago* – vague; something wandering, fluctuating, undefinable, undetainable, moving hither and thither at its own sweet will and pleasure, in accordance with what it feels. It overdoes nothing and falls short of nothing; for itself is nothing but the outward expression of an inward grace. You perceive it in all genuine lyrical compositions, of whatever degree, and indeed in all compositions that sing or speak with true musical impulse, in whatsoever measure, in the effusions of Burns, of Ben Jonson, of Beaumont and Fletcher, of Allan Ramsay, of Metastasio, of Coleridge; and again in those of Dryden, of Spenser, of Chaucer, of Ariosto; in poems however long, and in passages however seemingly unlyrical; for it is one of the popular, and I am afraid, generally speaking, critical mistakes, in regard to rhymed verse, that in narrative and heroic poems there is nothing wanting to the music, provided the line or the couplet be flowing, and the general impression not rude or weak; whereas the best couplet, however admirable in itself and worthy of quotation, forms, but one link in the chain of the music to which it belongs. Poems of any length must consist of whole strains of couplets, whole sections and successions of them, brief or prolonged, all as distinct from one another and complete in

76

themselves as the *adagios* and *andantes* of symphonies and sonatas, each commencing in the tone and obvious spirit of commencement, proceeding through as great a variety of accents, stops, and pauses as the notes and phrases of any other musical composition, and coming at an equally fit moment to a close.

Enough stress has never yet been laid on the analogies between musical and poetical composition. All poetry used formerly to be sung; and poets still speak of 'singing' what they write. Petrarch used to 'try his sonnets on the lute'; that is to say, to examine them in their musical relations, in order to see how they and musical requirement went together; and a chapter of poetical narrative is called to this day a canto, or chant. Every distinct section or paragraph of a long poem ought to form a separate, interwoven, and varied melody; and every very short poem should, to a fine ear, be a still more obvious melody of the same sort, in order that its brevity may contain as much worth as is possible, and show that the poet never forgets the reverence due to his art.

I have sometimes thought that if Chaucer could have heard compositions like those of Coleridge's 'Christabel', he might have doubted whether theirs was not the best of all modes and measures for reducing a narrative to its most poetic element, and so producing the quintessence of a story. And for stories not very long, not very substantial in their adventures, and of a nature more imaginary than credible, so they might be. But for narrative poetry in general, for epic in particular, and for stories of any kind that are deeply to affect us as creatures of flesh and blood and human experience, there is nothing for a sustained and serious interest comparable with our old heroic measure, whether in blank verse or rhyme, in couplet or in stanza. An epic poem written in the 'Christabel', or any other brief lyrical measure, would acquire, in the course of perusal, a comparative tone of levity, an air of too great an airiness. The matter would turn to something like not being in earnest, and the matter resemble a diet made of all essences. We should miss *pièces de resistance* and the homely, but sacred pabulum of 'our daily bread'. You could as soon fancy a guitar put in place of a church organ as an *Iliad* or *Paradise Lost* written in that manner. You would associate with it no tone of Scripture, nothing of the religious solemnity which Chaucer has so justly been said to impart to his pathetic stories. When poor *Griselda*, repudiated by her husband, and about to return to her father's cottage, puts off the clothes which she had worn as the consort of a great noble, she says,

> My lord, ye wot that in my father's place,
> Ye did me strip out of my poorĕ weed,
> And richĕly me cladden of your grace.
> To you brought I nought ellĕs, out of dreed, [*else   doubt*
> But faith, and nakedness, and maidenheed;
> And here again my clothing I restore,
> And eke my wedding-ring for evermore.
>
> The remnant of your jewels ready be
> Within your chamber, dare I safely sayn;
> 'Naked out of my father's house (quoth she) [*say*
> I came, and naked must I turn again.'³

This quotation from the Bible⁴ would have been injured by a shorter measure.

Griselda, in words most proper and affecting, but which cannot so well be quoted apart from the entire story, goes on to say that she must not deprive of every one of its clothes the body which had been made sacred by motherhood. She tells the father of her children that it is not fit she should be seen by the people in that condition.

> Wherefore I you pray,
> *Let me not like a worm go by the way.*

This is one of the most imploring and affecting lines that ever were written. It is also most beautifully modulated, though not at all after the fashion of the once all in all 'smooth' couplet. But the masterly accents throughout it, particularly the emphasis on 'worm', would have wanted room, and could have made no such earnest appeal, in a measure of less length and solemnity.

Irony itself gains by this measure. There is no sarcasm in *Hudibras*, exquisite as its sarcasm is, comparable for energy of tone and manner with Dryden's denunciation (I do not say just denunciation) of every species of priest.[5] I allude to the last four lines of the following passage:

> Thus worn, or weaken'd, well or ill content,
> Submit they must to David's government,
> Impoverish'd, and depriv'd of all command,
> Their taxes doubled as they lost their land,
> And what was harder yet to flesh and blood,
> Their gods disgrac'd, and burnt like common wood.
> This set the heathen priesthood in a flame;
> For priests of all religions are the same.
> *Of whatsoe'er descent their godhead be,*
> *Stock, stone, or other homely pedigree,*
> *In his defence his servants are as bold,*
> *As if he had been born of beaten gold.*[6]

It is worth the while of a student in versification to consider those four lines. They are perfect in music, expression, and force. The last, in particular, is a model, both for the image and the treatment; the image new, apposite, and surprising; the place in which it is put giving musical fulness to the cadence; its utterance bold, strong, and beautiful to the last degree, both of melody and power. The *b*'s beat it as if it was on an anvil; as if the gold they speak of were under their hammers; and the variety and *toning* of the vowels gives sweetness to the *bangs*. Mark the variety of accent which the poet has put into the space of four lines, and the strength which the slight sound on the last syllable of *pedigree* gives to the word *bold*, in the line ensuing:

> Of whatsoe'er descent their gòdhead be,
> Stòck, stòne, or òther hòmely pèdigree,
> In his defence his servants are as bòld,
> As if he had been bòrn of bèaten gòld.

I have dwelt more than is customary on the musical portion of the subject of poetry, for two reasons: first, because, as I have before intimated, it has a greater connection than is commonly thought, both with the spiritual and with the substantial portions of the art; and second, because, as I have asserted and am prepared to show, versification, or the various mode of uttering that music, has been neglected among us to a degree which is not a little remarkable, considering what an abundance of poets this country has produced.

England, it is true, is not a musical country; at any rate not yet, whatever its new trainers may do for it. But it is a very poetical country, *minus* this requisite of poetry; and it seems strange that the deficit should be corporately, as well as nationally characteristic. It might have been imagined that superiority in the one respect would have been accompanied by superiority in the other; that they who excelled the majority of their countrymen in poetical perception, would have excelled them in musical. Is the want the same as that which has made us inferior to other great nations in the art of painting? Are we geographically, commercially, statistically [inferior], or how is it that we are less gifted than other nations with those perceptions of the pleasurable which qualify people to excel as painters and musicians? It is observable that our poetry, compared with that of other countries, is deficient in animal spirits.

At all events, it is this ignorance of the necessity of the whole round of the elements of poetry for the production of a perfect poetical work and the non-perception, at the same time, of the two-fold fact that there is no such work in existence, and that the absence of no single element of poetry hinders the other elements from compounding a work truly poetical of its kind, which at different periods of literature produce so many defective and peremptory judgments respecting the exclusive right of this or that species of poetry to be called poetry. In Chaucer's time, there were probably Chaucerophilists who would see no poetry in any other man's writing. Sir Walter Ralegh, nevertheless, who, it might be supposed, would have been an enthusiastic admirer of the Knight's and Squire's Tales, openly said that he counted no English poetry of any value but that of Spenser. In Cowley's time, 'thinking' was held to be the all in all of poetry: poems were to be crammed full of thoughts, otherwise intellectual activity was wanting; and hence, nothing was considered poetry, in the highest sense of the term, that did not resemble the metaphysics of Cowley. His 'language of the heart', which has survived them, went comparatively for nothing. When the Puritans brought sentiment into discredit, nothing was considered comparable, in any species of poetry, with the noble music and robust sensuous perception of Dryden. Admirable poet as he was, he was thought then, and long afterwards, to be far more admirable – indeed, the sole 'Great high-priest of all the Nine'.

Then 'sense' became the all in all; and because Pope wrote a great deal of exquisite sense, adorned with wit and fancy, he was pronounced, and long considered, literally, the greatest poet that England had seen. A healthy breeze from the unsophisticate region of the Old English Ballads suddenly roused the whole poetical elements into play, restoring a sense of the combined requisites of imagination, of passion, of simple speaking, of music, of animal spirits, etc., not omitting, of course, the true thinking which all sound feeling implies; and though, with the prevailing grave tendency of the English muse, some portions of these poetical requisites came more into play than others, and none of our poets, either since or before, have combined them all as Chaucer and Shakspeare did, yet it would as ill become poets or critics to ignore any one of them in favour of exclusive pretensions on the part of any others, as it would to say that all the music, and animal spirits, and comprehensiveness might be taken out of those two wonderful men, and they remain just what they were.

To think that there can be no poetry, properly so called, where there is anything 'artificial', where there are conventionalisms of style, where facts are simply related without obviously imaginative treatment, or where manner, for its own sake, is held to be a thing of any account in its presentation of matter, is showing as limited a state of critical perception as that of the opposite

onventional faction, who can see no poetry out of the pale of
eceived forms, classical associations, or total subjections of
piritual to material treatment. It is a case of imperfect sympathy
n both sides – of incompetency to discern and enjoy in another
vhat they have no corresponding tendency to in themselves. It
s often a complexional case; perhaps always so, more or less: for
vriters and critics, like all other human creatures, are physically
s well as morally disposed to be what they become. It is the
ntire man that writes and thinks, and not merely the head. His
eg has often as much to do with it as his head – the state of his
alves, his vitals, and his nerves.

There is a charming line in Chaucer: 'Uprose the sun, and
prose Emily.'[7] Now here are two simple matters of fact, which
iappen to occur simultaneously. The sun rises, and the lady rises
t the same time. Well, what is there in that, some demanders
f imaginative illustration will say? Nothing, answers one, but
n hyperbole. Nothing, says another, but a conceit. It is a mere
ommonplace turn of gallantry, says a third. On the contrary, it
s the reverse of all this. It is pure morning freshness, enthusiasm,
nd music. Writers, no doubt, may repeat it till it becomes a
ommonplace, but that is another matter. Its first sayer, the great
oet, sees the brightest of material creatures, and the beautifulest
f human creatures, rising at dawn at the same time. He feels
he impulse strong upon him to do justice to the appearance of
oth; and with gladness in his face, and music on his tongue,
epeating the accent on a repeated syllable, and dividing the
hythm into two equal parts, in order to leave nothing undone to
how the merit on both sides, and the rapture of his impartiality,
ie utters, for all time, his enchanting record.

Now it requires animal spirits, or a thoroughly loving nature,
o enjoy that line completely; and yet, on looking well into it, it
vill be found to contain (by implication) simile, analogy, and,
ndeed, every other form of imaginative expression, apart from
hat of direct illustrative words; which, in such cases, may be
alled needless commentary. The poet lets nature speak for
ierself. He points to the two beautiful objects before us, and is

content with simply hailing them in their combination.

In all cases where Nature should thus be left to speak for herself (and they are neither mean nor few cases, but many and great) the imaginative faculty, which some think to be totally suspended at such times, is, on the contrary, in full activity, keeping aloof all irrelevancies and impertinence, and thus showing how well it understands its great mistress. When *Lady Macbeth* says she should have murdered *Duncan* herself,

> Had he not resembled
> Her father as he slept,

she said neither more nor less than what a poor criminal said long afterwards, and quite unaware of the passage, when brought before a magistrate from a midnight scuffle in a barge on the Thames – 'I should have killed him, if he had not looked so like my father while he was sleeping.' Shakspeare made poetry of the thought by putting it into verse – into modulation; but he would not touch it otherwise. He reverenced Nature's own simple, awful, and sufficing suggestion too much to add a syllable to it for the purpose of showing off his subtle powers of imaginative illustration. And with no want of due reverence to Shakspeare, be it said that it is a pity he did not act invariably with the like judgment – that he suffered thought to crowd upon thought, where the first feeling was enough. So, what can possibly be imagined simpler, finer, completer, less wanting anything beyond itself, than the line in which poor old *Lear*, unable to relieve himself with his own trembling fingers, asks the bystander to open his waistcoat for him – not forgetting, in the midst of his anguish, to return him thanks for so doing, like a gentleman: 'Pray you undo this button. – Thank you, Sir.' The poet here presents us with two matters of fact, in their simplest and apparently most prosaical form; yet, when did ever passion or imagination speak more intensely? and this, purely because he has let them alone?

There is another line in Chaucer which seems to be still plainer matter of fact, with no imagination in it of any kind, apart from the simple necessity of imagining the fact itself. It is in the story of the Tartar king, which Milton wished to have had completed. The king has been feasting and is moving from the feast to a ball-room: 'Before him goeth the loud minstrelsy.'[8] Now, what is there in this line (it might be asked) which might not have been said in plain prose? which indeed is not prose? The king is preceded by his musicians, playing loudly. What is there in that?

Well, there is something even in that, if the prosers who demand so much help to their perceptions could but see it. But verse fetches it out and puts it in its proper state of movement. The line itself, being a line of verse, and therefore a musical movement, becomes processional, and represents the royal train in action. The word 'goeth', which a less imaginative writer would have rejected in favour of something which he took to be more spiritual and uncommon, is the soul of the continuity of the movement. It is put, accordingly, in its most emphatic place. And the word 'loud' is suggestive at once of royal power, and of the mute and dignified serenity, superior to that manifestation of it, with which the king follows. '*Before* him goeth the loud minstrelsy.' Any reader who does not recognise the stately 'go', and altogether noble sufficingness of that line, may rest assured that thousands of the beauties of poetry will remain forever undiscovered by him, let him be helped by as many thoughts and images as he may.

So in a preceding passage where the same musicians are mentioned.

> And so befell, that after the third course,
> While that this King sat thus in his nobley, –   [*nobleness*
> Hearing his minstrallés their thingés play
> Before him at his board deliciously,
> In at the hallé-door all suddenly
> There came a knight upon a steed of brass,
> And in his hand a broad mirror of glass;
> Upon his thumb he had of gold a ring,
> And by his side a naked sword hanging,

And up he rideth to the highé board. –
In all the hallé n'as there spoke a word   [*was not*
For marvel of this knight. – Him to behold
Full busily they waited, young and old.[9]

In some of these lines, what would otherwise be prose becomes, by the musical feeling, poetry. The king, 'sitting in his nobleness', is an imaginative picture. The word 'deliciously' is a venture of animal spirits, which, in a modern writer, some critic would pronounce to be affected, or too familiar; but the enjoyment, and even incidental appropriateness and *relish* of it, will be obvious to finer senses. And in the pause in the middle of the last couplet but one, and that in the course of the first line of its successor, examples were given by this supposed unmusical old poet, of some of the highest refinements of versification.

The secret of musical, as of all other feeling, lies in the depths of the harmonious adjustments of our nature; and a chord touched in any one of them vibrates with the rest. In the Queen's beautiful letter to Mr Sidney Herbert, about the sufferers in the Crimea, the touching words, 'those poor noble wounded and sick men', would easily, and with perfectly poetical sufficiency, flow into verse. Chaucer, with his old English dissyllable, *poore*, (more piteous, because lingering in the sound), would have found in them a verse ready made to his hand – 'Those poorĕ noble wounded and sick men.'

The passage is in fact just like one of his own verses, sensitive, earnest, strong, simple, full of truth, full of harmonious sympathy. Many a manly eye will it moisten; many a poor soldier, thus acknowledged to be a 'noble', will it pay for many a pang. What, if transferred to verse, would it need from any other kind of imaginative treatment? What, indeed, could it receive but injury? And yet, to see what is said by the demanders, on every possible poetical occasion, of perpetual commentating thoughts and imaginative analogies, one must conclude that they would pronounce it to be wholly unfit for poetry, unless something very fine were added about 'poor', something very fine about 'noble', something very fine about 'wounded', and something very fine about 'sick'; a process by which our sympathy with the suffering heroes would come to nothing in comparison with our astonishment at the rhetoric of the eulogizers – which, indeed, is a 'consummation' that writers of this description would seem to desire.

Of all the definitions which have been given to poetry, the best is that which pronounces it to be 'geniality, singing'. I think, but am not sure, that it is Lamb's; perhaps it is Coleridge's. I had not seen it, or, if I had, had lost all recollection of it when I wrote the book called *Imagination and Fancy*; otherwise I would have substituted it for the definition given in that book; for it comprehends, by implication, all which is there said respecting the different classes and degrees of poetry, and excludes, at the same time, whatsoever does not properly come within the limits of the thing defined.

Geniality, thus considered, is not to be understood in its common limited acceptation of a warm and flowing spirit of companionship. It includes that and every other motive to poetic utterance; but it resumes its great primal meaning of the power of productiveness; that power from which the word Genius is derived, and which falls in so completely with the meaning of the word Poet itself, which is Maker. The poet makes, or produces, because he has a desire to do so; and what he produces is found to be worthy, in proportion as time shows a desire to retain it. As all trees are trees, whatever be the different degrees of their importance, so all poets are poets whose productions have a character of their own, and take root in the ground of national acceptance. The poet sings, because he is excited, and because whatsoever he does must be moulded into a shape of beauty. If imagination predominates in him, and it is of the true kind, and he loves the exercise of it better than the fame, he stands a chance of being a poet of the highest order, but not of the only order. If fancy predominates, and the fancy is of the true kind, he is no less a poet in kind, though inferior in degree. If thought predominate, he is a contemplative poet: if a variety of these faculties in combination, he is various accordingly; less great, perhaps, in each individually, owing to the divided interest which he takes in the claim upon his attention; but far greater, if equally great in all. Nevertheless, he does not hinder his less accomplished brethren from being poets. There is a talk of confining the appellation poet, to the inspired poet. But who and what is the inspired poet? Inspired means 'breathed into'; that is to say, by some superior influence. But how is not Dryden breathed into as well as Chaucer? Milton as well as Shakspeare? or Pope as well as Milton? The flute, though out of all comparison with the organ, is still an instrument 'breathed into'. The only question is whether it is breathed into finely, and so as to render it a flute extraordinary; whether the player is a man of genius after his kind, not to be mechanically made. You can no more make a Burns than a Homer; no more the author of a *Rape of the Lock* than the author of *Paradise Lost*. If you could, you would have Burnses as plentiful as blackberries, and as many 'Rapes of the Lock' as books of mightier pretension, that are forever coming out and going into oblivion. Meantime, *The Rape of the Lock* remains, and why? Because it is an inspired poem; a poem as truly inspired by the genius of wit and fancy, as the gravest and grandest that ever was written was inspired by passion and imagination.

This is the secret of a great, national, book-reading fact, the existence of which has long puzzled exclusives in poetry; to wit, the never-failing demand in all civilized countries for successive publications of bodies of collected verse, called English or British Poets, Italian Poets, French Poets, Spanish Poets, etc. – collections which stand upon no ceremony whatever with exclusive predilections, but tend to include every thing that has attained poetical repute, and are generally considered to be what they ought to be in proportion as they are copious. Poetasters are sometimes admitted for poets; and poets are sometimes missed, because they have been taken for poetasters. But, upon the whole, the chance of excess is preferred: and the preference is well founded; for the whole system is founded on a judicious instinct. Feelings are nature's reasons; communities often feel better than individuals reason; and they feel better in this instance. Hence Popes and

Drydens never cease to be found in collections of English verse, as well as Spensers and Miltons: hence Butlers and Swifts, as well as Popes and Drydens: hence all writers in verse, who have any character of their own whatsoever, and whose productions, having once become acquainted with them, readers who love 'geniality' of any kind, 'singing', would miss. Butler could not have said so well in prose what he has said in verse; and hence he felt an impulse to speak in verse, and he is a wit-poet accordingly. The flow of Swift's wit, of Prior's, of Green's[10] (pity that the stream in the two former is so often polluted) would have wanted half its force and effect, without the compression given to it by verse. They felt this; they were as much inclined to the song of it as to the substance; and hence they also are wits who 'sing' – poets, after their kind, not to be left out of the collections. . . .

1855

S.T. Coleridge

Coleridge was as little fitted for action as Lamb, but on a different account. His person was of a good height, but as sluggish and solid as the other's was light and fragile. He had, perhaps, suffered it to look old before its time, for want of exercise. His hair was white at fifty; and as he generally dressed in black, and had a very tranquil demeanour, his appearance was gentlemanly, and for several years before his death was reverend. Nevertheless, there was something invincibly young in the look of his face. It was round and fresh-coloured, with agreeable features, and an open, indolent, good-natured mouth. This boy-like expression was very becoming in one who dreamed and speculated as he did when he was really a boy, and who passed his life apart from the rest of the world, with a book, and his flowers. His forehead was prodigious – a great piece of placid marble; and his fine eyes, in which all the activity of his mind seemed to concentrate, moved under it with a sprightly ease, as if it was pastime to them to carry all that thought.

And it was pastime. Hazlitt said that Coleridge's genius appeared to him like a spirit, all head and wings, eternally floating about in the etherealities. He gave me a different impression. I fancied him a good-natured wizard, very fond of earth, and conscious of reposing with weight enough in his easy chair, but able to conjure his etherealities about him in the twinkling of an eye. He could also change them by thousands, and dismiss them as easily when his dinner came. It was a mighty intellect put upon a sensual body; and the reason why he did little more with it than talk and dream was, that it is agreeable to such a body to do little else. I do not mean that Coleridge was a sensualist in an ill sense. He was capable of too many innocent pleasures to take any pleasure in the way that a man of the world would take it. The idlest things he did would have had a warrant. But if all the senses, in their time, did not find lodging in that humane plenitude of his, never believe that they did in Thomson or in Boccaccio. Two affirmatives in him made a negative. He was very metaphysical and very corporeal; so in mooting everything, he said (so to speak) nothing. His brains pleaded all sorts of questions before him, and he heard them with too much impartiality (his spleen not giving him any trouble), that he thought he might as well sit in his easy chair and hear them for ever, without coming to a conclusion. It has been said (indeed, he said himself) that he took opium to deaden the sharpness of his cogitations. I will venture to affirm, that if he ever took anything to deaden a sensation within him, it was for no greater or more marvellous a reason than other people take it; which is, because they do not take enough exercise, and so plague their heads with their livers. Opium, perhaps, might have settled an uneasiness of this sort in Coleridge, as it did in a much less man with a much greater body – the Shadwell of Dryden.[1] He would then resume his natural ease, and sit, and be happy, till the want of exercise must be again supplied. The vanity of criticism, like all other vanities, except that of dress (which, so far, has an involuntary philosophy n it), is always forgetting that we are half made up of body. Hazlitt was angry with Coleridge for not being as zealous in behalf of progress as he used to be when young. I was sorry for it, too; and if other men as well as Hazlitt had not kept me in heart, I should have feared that the world was destined to be for ever lost, for want either of perseverance or calmness. But Coleridge had less right to begin his zeal in favour of liberty than he had to leave it off. He should have bethought himself, first, whether he had the courage not to get fat.

As to the charge against him, of eternally probing the depths of his own mind, and trying what he could make of them beyond the ordinary pale of logic and philosophy, surely there was no harm in a man taking this new sort of experiment upon him, whatever little chance there may have been of his doing anything with it. Coleridge, after all, was but one man, though an extraordinary man: his faculties inclined him to the task, and were suitable to it; and it is impossible to say what new worlds may be laid open, some day or other, by this apparently hopeless process. The fault of Coleridge, like that of all thinkers indisposed to action, was, that he was too content with things as they were, – at least, too fond of thinking that old corruptions were full of good things, if the world did but understand them. Now, here was the dilemma; for it required an understanding like his own to refine upon and turn them to good as he might do; and what the world requires is not metaphysical refinement, but a hearty use of good sense. Coleridge, indeed, could refine his meaning so as to accommodate it with good-nature to every one that came across him; and, doubtless, he found more agreement of intention among people of different opinions, than they themselves were aware of; which it was good to let them see. But when not enchained by his harmony, they fell asunder again, or went and committed the greatest absurdities for want of the subtle connecting tie; as was seen in the books of Mr Irving,[2] who, eloquent in one page, and reasoning in a manner that a child ought to be ashamed of in the next, thought to avail himself, in times like these, of the old menacing tones of damnation, without being

90

considered a quack or an idiot, purely because Coleridge had shown him, last Friday, that damnation was not what its preachers took it for. With the same subtlety and good-nature of interpretation, Coleridge would persuade a deist that he was a Christian, and an atheist that he believed in God: all which would be very good, if the world could get on by it, and not remain stationary; but, meanwhile, millions are wretched with having too little to eat, and thousands with having too much; and these subtleties are like people talking in their sleep, when they should be up and helping.

However, if the world is to remain always as it is, give me to all eternity new talk of Coleridge, and new essays of Charles Lamb. They will reconcile it beyond all others: and that is much.

Coleridge was fat, and began to lament, in very delightful verses, that he was getting infirm. There was no old age in his verses. I heard him one day, under the Grove at Highgate, repeat one of his melodious lamentations, as he walked up and down, his voice undulating in a stream of music, and his regrets of youth sparkling with visions ever young. At the same time he did me the honour to show me that he did not think so ill of all modern liberalism as some might suppose, denouncing the pretensions of the money-getting in a style which I should hardly venture upon and never could equal; and asking with a triumphant eloquence what chastity itself were worth, if it were a casket, not to keep love in, but hate, and strife, and worldliness? On the same occasion, he built up a metaphor out of a flower, in a style surpassing the famous passage in Milton; denouncing it from its root in religious mystery, and carrying it up into the bright, consummate flower, 'the bridal chamber of reproductiveness'. Of all 'the Muse's mysteries', he was as great a high priest as Spenser; and Spenser himself might have gone to Highgate to hear him talk, and thank him for his *Ancient Mariner*. His voice did not always sound very sincere; but perhaps the humble and deprecating tone of it, on those occasions, was out of consideration for the infirmities of his hearers, rather than produced by his own. He recited his *Kubla Khan* one morning to Lord Byron, in his lordship's house in Piccadilly, when I happened to be in another room. I remember the other's coming away from him, highly struck with his poem, and saying how wonderfully he talked. This was the impression of everybody who heard him.

It is no secret that Coleridge lived in the Grove at Highgate with a friendly family,[3] who had sense and kindness enough to know that they did themselves honour by looking after the comfort of such a man. His room looked upon a delicious prospect of wood and meadow, with coloured gardens under the window, like an embroidery to the mantle. I thought, when I first saw it, that he had taken up his dwelling-place like an abbot. Here he cultivated his flowers, and had a set of birds for his pensioners, who came to breakfast with him. He might have been seen taking his daily stroll up and down, with his black coat and white locks, with a book in his hand; and was a great acquaintance of the little children. His main occupation, I believe, was reading. He loved to read old folios, and to make old voyages with Purchas and Marco Polo; the seas being in good visionary condition, and the vessel well stocked with botargoes.*

* For a more critical summary of my opinions respecting Coleridge's poetry (which I take upon the whole to have been the finest of its time; that is to say, the most quintessential, the most purely emanating from imaginative feeling, unadulterated by 'thoughts' and manner), the reader may, if he pleases, consult *Imagination and Fancy*.

Autobiography
1859

Charles Lamb

Lamb was a humanist, in the most universal sense of the term. His imagination was not great, and he also wanted sufficient heat and music to render his poetry as good as his prose; but as a prose writer, and within the wide circuit of humanity, no man ever took a more complete range than he. He had felt, thought, and suffered so much, that he literally had intolerance for nothing; and he never seemed to have it, but when he supposed the sympathies of men, who might have known better, to be imperfect. He was a wit and an observer of the first order, as far as the world around him was concerned, and society in its existing state; for as to anything theoretical or transcendental, no man ever had less care for it, or less power. To take him out of habit and convention, however tolerant he was to those who could speculate beyond them, was to put him into an exhausted receiver, or to send him naked, shivering, and driven to shatters, through the regions of space and time. He was only at his ease in the old arms of humanity; and humanity loved and comforted him like one of its wisest, though weakest children. His life had experienced great and peculiar sorrows; but he kept up a balance between those and his consolations, by the goodness of his heart, and the everwilling sociality of his humour; though, now and then, as if he would cram into one moment the spleen of years, he would throw out a startling and morbid subject for reflection, perhaps in no better shape than a pun; for he was a great punster. It was a levity that relieved the gravity of his thoughts and kept them from falling too heavily earthwards.

Lamb was under the middle size, and of fragile make; but with a head as fine as if it had been carved on purpose. He had a very weak stomach. Three glasses of wine would put him in as lively a condition as can only be wrought in some men by as many bottles; which subjected him to mistakes on the part of the inconsiderate.

Lamb's essays, especially those collected under the signature of *Elia*, will take their place among the daintiest productions of English *wit-melancholy*, – an amiable melancholy being the groundwork of them, and serving to throw out their delicate flowers of wit and character with the greater nicety. Nor will they be liked the less for a sprinkle of old language, which was natural in him by reason of his great love of the old English writers. Shakspeare himself might have read them, and Hamlet have quoted them.

Table Talk
1851

from Lord Byron

The first time I saw Lord Byron, he was rehearsing the part of Leander, under the auspices of Mr Jackson the prize-fighter. It was in the river Thames, before he went to Greece. I had been bathing, and was standing on the floating machine adjusting my clothes, when I noticed a respectable-looking manly person, who was eyeing something at a distance. This was Mr Jackson waiting for his pupil. The latter was swimming with somebody for a wager. I forget what his tutor said of him; but he spoke in terms of praise. I saw nothing in Lord Byron at that time, but a young man who, like myself, had written a bad volume of poems; and though I had sympathy with him on this account, and more respect for his rank than I was willing to suppose, my sympathy was not an agreeable one; so, contenting myself with seeing his Lordship's head bob up and down in the water, like a buoy, I came away.

Lord Byron was afterwards pleased to regret, that I had not stayed. He told me, that the sight of my volume at Harrow had been one of his incentives to write verses, and that he had had the same passion for friendship that I had displayed in it. To my astonishment, he quoted some of the lines, and would not hear me speak ill of them. This was when I was in prison, where I first became personally acquainted with his Lordship. His harbinger was Moore.[1] Moore told me, that, besides liking my politics, he liked 'The Feast of the Poets', and would be glad to make my acquaintance. I said I felt myself highly flattered, and should be proud to entertain his Lordship as well as a poor patriot could. He was accordingly invited to dinner. His friend only stipulated, that there should be 'plenty of fish and vegetables for the noble bard', his Lordship at that time being Brahminical in his eating. He came, and we passed a very pleasant afternoon, talking of books, and school, and the Reverend Mr Bowles;[2] of the pastoral innocence of whose conversation some anecdotes were related, that would have much edified the spirit of Pope, had it been in the room.

I saw nothing at first but single-hearted and agreeable qualities in Lord Byron. My wife, with the quicker eyes of a woman, was inclined to doubt them. Visiting me one day, when I had a friend with me, he seemed uneasy, and asked without ceremony when he should find me alone. My friend, who was a man of taste and spirit, and the last in the world to intrude his acquaintance, was not bound to go away because another person had come in; and besides, he naturally felt anxious to look at so interesting a visitor; which was paying the latter a compliment. But his Lordship's will was disturbed, and he vented his spleen accordingly. I took it at the time for a piece of simplicity, blinded perhaps by the flattery insinuated towards myself; but my wife was right. Lord Byron's nature, from the first, contained that mixture of disagreeable with pleasanter qualities, which I had afterwards but too much occasion to recognize. He subsequently called on me in the prison several times, and used to bring books for my *Story of Rimini*, which I was then writing. He would not let the footman bring them in. He would enter with a couple of quartos under his arm; and give you to understand, that he was prouder of being a friend and a man of letters, than a lord. It was thus that by flattering one's vanity, he persuaded us of his own freedom from it; for he could see very well, that I had more value for lords than I supposed.

...He was a warm politician, and thought himself earnest in the cause of liberty. His failure in the House of Lords is well known. He was very candid about it; said he was much frightened, and should never be able to do any thing that way. Lords of all parties came about him, and consoled him; he particularly mentioned Lord Sidmouth, as being unaffectedly kind. When I left prison, I was too ill to return his visits. He pressed me very much to go to the theatre with him; but illness, and the dread of committing my critical independence, alike prevented me. His Lordship was one of a management that governed Drury-lane Theatre at that time, and that made a sad business of their direction, as amateur-managers have always done. He got nothing by it but petty vexations, and a good deal of scandal....

95

Lord Byron's face was handsome; eminently so in some respects. He had a mouth and chin fit for Apollo; and when I first saw him, there were both lightness and energy all over his aspect. But his countenance did not improve with age, and there were always some defects in it. The jaw was too big for the upper part. It had all the wilfulness of a despot in it. The animal predominated over the intellectual part of his head, inasmuch as the face altogether was large in proportion to the skull. The eyes also were set too near one another; and the nose, though handsome in itself, had the appearance when you saw it closely in front, of being grafted on the face, rather than growing properly out of it. His person was very handsome, though terminating in lameness, and tending to fat and effeminacy; which makes me remember what a hostile fair one objected to him, namely, that he had little beard; a fault which, on the other hand, was thought by another lady, not hostile, to add to the divinity of his aspect, – *imberbis Apollo*. His lameness was only in one foot, the left; and it was so little visible to casual notice, that as he lounged about a room (which he did in such a manner as to screen it) it was hardly perceivable. But it was a real and even a sore lameness. Much walking upon it fevered and hurt it. It was a shrunken foot, a little twisted. This defect unquestionably mortified him exceedingly, and helped to put sarcasm and misanthropy into his taste of life. Unfortunately, the usual thoughtlessness of schoolboys made him feel it bitterly at Harrow. He would walk, and find his leg in a tub of water. The reader will see in the correspondence at the end of this memoir,[3] how he felt it, whenever it was libelled; and in Italy, the only time I ever knew it mentioned, he did not like the subject, and hastened to change it. His handsome person so far rendered the misfortune greater, as it pictured to him all the occasions on which he might have figured in the eyes of company; and doubtless this was a great reason, why he had no better address. On the other hand, instead of losing him any real regard or admiration, his lameness gave a touching character to both. Certainly no reader would have liked him, or woman loved him, the less, for the thought of this single contrast to his superiority. But the very defect had taught him to be impatient with deficiency. Good God! when I think of these things, and of the common weaknesses of society, as at present constituted, I feel as if I could shed tears over the most willing of my resentments, much more over the most unwilling, and such as I never intended to speak of; nor could any thing have induced me to give a portrait of Lord Byron and his infirmities, if I had not been able to say at the end of it, that his faults were not his own, and that we must seek the causes of them in mistakes common to us all. What is delightful to us in his writings will still remain so, if we are wise; and what ought not to be, will not only cease to be perilous, but be useful. Faults which arise from an exuberant sociality, like those of Burns, may safely be left to themselves. They at once explain themselves by their natural candour, and carry an advantage with them; because any thing is advantageous in the long run to society, which tends to break up their selfishness. But doctrines, or half-doctrines, or whatever else they may be, which tend to throw individuals upon themselves, and overcast them at the same time with scorn and alienation, it is as well to see traced to their sources. In comparing notes, humanity gets wise; and certainly the wiser it gets, it will not be the less modest or humane, whether it has to find fault, or to criticise the fault-finder.

I believe if any body could have done good to Lord Byron, it was Goethe and his correspondence. It was a pity he did not live to have more of it. Goethe might possibly have enabled him, as he wished he could, 'to know himself', and do justice to the yearnings after the good and beautiful inseparable from the nature of genius. But the danger was, that he would have been influenced as much by the rank and reputation of that great man, as by the reconciling nobleness of his philosophy; and personal intercourse with him would have spoilt all. Lord Byron's nature was mixed up with too many sophistications to receive a proper impression from any man: and he would have been jealous, if he once took it in his head that the other was thought to be his superior.

Lord Byron had no conversation, properly speaking. He could not interchange ideas or information with you, as a man of letters is expected to do. His thoughts required the conversation of silence and study to bring them to a head; and they deposited the amount in the shape of a stanza. His acquaintance with books was very circumscribed. The same personal experience, however, upon which he very properly drew for his authorship, might have rendered him a companion more interesting by far than men who could talk better; and the great reason why his conversation disappointed you was, not that he had not any thing to talk about, but that he was haunted with a perpetual affectation, and could not talk sincerely. It was by fits only that he spoke with any gravity, or made his extraordinary disclosures; and at no time did you well know what to believe. The rest was all quip and crank, not of the pleasantest kind, and equally distant from simplicity or wit. The best thing to say of it was, that he knew playfulness to be consistent with greatness; and the worst, that he thought every thing in him was great, even to his vulgarities.

Mr Shelley said of him, that he never made you laugh to your own content. This, however, was said latterly, after my friend had been disappointed by a close intimacy. Mr Shelley's opinion of his natural powers in every respect was great; and there is reason to believe, that Lord Byron never talked with any man to so much purpose as he did with him. He looked upon him as his most admiring listener; and probably was never less under the influence of affectation. If he could have got rid of this and his title, he would have talked like a man; not like a mere man of the town, or a great spoilt schoolboy. It is not to be concluded, that his jokes were not now and then very happy, or that admirers of his Lordship, who paid him visits, did not often go away more admiring. I am speaking of his conversation in general, and of the impression it made upon you, compared with what was to be expected from a man of wit and experience.

He had a delicate white hand, of which he was proud; and he attracted attention to it by rings. He thought a hand of this description almost the only mark remaining now-a-days of a gentleman;

of which it certainly is not, nor of a lady either; though a coarse one implies handiwork. He often appeared holding a handkerchief, upon which his jewelled fingers lay imbedded, as in a picture. He was as fond of fine linen, as a quaker; and had the remnant of his hair oiled and trimmed with all the anxiety of a Sardanapalus.

The visible character to which this effeminacy gave rise appears to have indicated itself as early as his travels in the Levant, where the Grand Signior is said to have taken him for a woman in disguise. But he had tastes of a more masculine description. He was fond of swimming to the last, and used to push out to a good distance in the Gulf of Genoa. He was also, as I have before mentioned, a good horseman; and he liked to have a great dog or two about him, which is not a habit observable in timid men. Yet I doubt greatly whether he was a man of courage. I suspect, that personal anxiety, coming upon a constitution unwisely treated, had no small hand in hastening his death in Greece.

Lord Byron and His Contemporaries
1828

from Mr Shelley

Mr Shelley, when he died, was in his thirtieth year. His figure was tall and slight, and his constitution consumptive. He was subject to violent spasmodic pains, which would sometimes force him to lie on the ground till they were over; but he had always a kind word to give to those about him, when his pangs allowed him to speak. In this organization, as well as in some other respects, he resembled the German poet, Schiller. Though well-turned, his shoulders were bent a little, owing to premature thought and trouble. The same causes had touched his hair with grey: and though his habits of temperance and exercise gave him a remarkable degree of strength, it is not supposed that he could have lived many years. He used to say, that he had lived three times as long as the calendar gave out; which he would prove, between jest and earnest, by some remarks on Time, 'That would have puzzled that stout Stagyrite'. Like the Stagyrite's, [Aristotle], his voice was high and weak. His eyes were large and animated, with a dash of wildness in them; his face small, but well-shaped, particularly the mouth and chin, the turn of which was very sensitive and graceful. His complexion was naturally fair and delicate, with a colour in the cheeks. He had brown hair, which, though tinged with grey, surmounted his face well, being in considerable quantity, and tending to a curl. His side-face upon the whole was deficient in strength, and his features would not have told well in a bust; but when fronting and looking at you attentively, his aspect had a certain seraphical character that would have suited a portrait of John the Baptist, or the angel whom Milton describes as holding a reed 'tipt with fire'. Nor would the most religious mind, had it known him, have objected to the comparison; for, with all his scepticism, Mr Shelley's disposition may be truly said to have been any thing but irreligious. A person of much eminence for piety in our times has well observed, that the greatest want of religious feeling is not to be found among the greatest infidels, but among those who never think of religion but as a matter of course. The leading feature of Mr Shelley's character, may be said to have been a natural piety. He was pious towards nature, towards his friends, towards the whole human race, towards the meanest insect in the forest. He did himself an injustice with the public, in using the popular name of the Supreme Being inconsiderately. He identified it solely with the most vulgar and tyrannical notions of a God made after the worst human fashion; and did not sufficiently reflect, that it was often used by a juster devotion to express a sense of the great Mover of the universe. An impatience in contradicting worldly and pernicious notions of a supernatural power, led his own aspirations to be misconstrued; for though, in the severity of his dialectics, and particularly in moments of despondency, he sometimes appeared to be hopeless of what he most desired, – and though

100

he justly thought, that a Divine Being would prefer the increase of benevolence and good before any praise, or even recognition of himself, (a reflection worth thinking of by the intolerant,) yet there was in reality no belief to which he clung with more fondness than that of some great pervading 'Spirit of Intellectual Beauty'; as may be seen in his aspirations on that subject. He said to me in the cathedral at Pisa, while the organ was playing, 'What a divine religion might be found out, if charity were really made the principle of it, instead of faith!'

Music affected him deeply. He had also a delicate perception of the beauties of sculpture. It is not one of the least evidences of his conscientious turn of mind, that with the inclination, and the power, to surround himself in Italy with all the graces of life, he made no sort of attempt that way; finding other use for his money, and not always satisfied with himself for indulging even in the luxury of a boat. When he bought elegancies of any kind, it was to give away. Boating was his great amusement. He loved the mixture of action and repose which he found in it; and delighted to fancy himself gliding away to Utopian isles, and bowers of enchantment. But he would give up any pleasure to do a deed of kindness. 'His life,' says Mrs Shelley, 'was spent in the contemplation of nature, in arduous study, or in acts of kindness and affection. He was an elegant scholar, and a profound metaphysician. Without possessing much scientific knowledge, he was unrivalled in the justness and extent of his observations on natural objects: he knew every plant by its name, and was familiar with the history and habits of every production of the earth: he could interpret, without a fault, each appearance in the sky; and the varied phenomena of heaven and earth filled him with deep emotion. He made his study and reading-room of the shadowed copse, the stream, the lake, and the waterfall' – *Preface* to his Posthumous Poems, p. 14. 'The comparative solitude,' observes the same lady, 'in which Mr Shelley lived, was the occasion that he was personally known to few; and his fearless enthusiasm in the cause which he considered the most sacred upon earth, the improvement of the moral and physical state of

101

mankind, was the chief reason why he, like other illustrious reformers, was pursued by hatred and calumny. No man was ever
more devoted than he to the endeavour of making those around
him happy; no man ever possessed friends more unfeignedly
attached to him. Before the critics contradict me, let them appeal
to any one who had ever known him. To see him was to love
him.' – *Ibid*. This is a high character, and I, for one, know it was
deserved. I should be glad to know, how many wives of Mr
Shelley's calumniators could say as much of their husbands; or
how many of the critics would believe them, if they did.

Mr Shelley's comfort was a sacrifice to the perpetual contradiction between the professions of society and their practice; between
'the shows of things and the desires of the mind'. Temperament
and early circumstances conspired to make him a reformer, at a
time of life when few begin to think for themselves; and it was
his misfortune, as far as immediate reputation was concerned,
that he was thrown upon society with a precipitancy and vehe-
mence, which rather startled them with fear for themselves, than
allowed them to become sensible of the love and zeal that impel-
led him. He was like a spirit that had darted out of its orb, and
found itself in another planet. I used to tell him that he had come
from the planet Mercury. When I heard of the catastrophe that
overtook him, it seemed as if this spirit, not sufficiently constituted like the rest of the world, to obtain their sympathy, yet
gifted with a double portion of love for all living things, had been
found dead in a solitary corner of the earth, its wings stiffened,
its warm heart cold; the relics of a misunderstood nature, slain
by the ungenial elements. . . .

Mr Shelley's poetry is invested with a dazzling and subtle
radiance, which blinds the common observer with light. Piercing
beyond this, we discover that the characteristics of his poetical
writings are an exceeding sympathy with the whole universe,
material and intellectual; an ardent desire to benefit his species;
an impatience of the tyrannies and superstitions that hold them
bound; and a regret that the power of one loving and enthusiastic
individual is not proportioned to his will, nor his good reception

with the world at all proportioned to his love. His poetry is either made up of all these feelings united, or is an attempt to escape from their pressure into the widest fields of imagination. I say an attempt, – because, as we have seen, escape he does not; and it is curious to observe how he goes pouring forth his baffled affections upon every object he can think of, bringing out its beauties and pretensions by the light of a radiant fancy, and resolved to do the whole detail of the universe a sort of poetical justice, in default of being able to make his fellow-creatures attend to justice political. From this arises the fault of his poetry, which is a want of massiveness, – of a proper distribution of light and shade. The whole is too full of glittering points; of images touched and illustrated alike, and brought out into the same prominence. He ransacks every thing like a bee, grappling with it in the same spirit of penetration and enjoyment, till you lose sight of the field he entered upon, in following him into his subtle recesses. He is also too fond, in his larger works, of repeating the same images drawn from the material universe and the sea. When he is obliged to give up these peculiarities, and to identify his feelings and experience with those of other people, as in his dramatic poems, the fault no longer exists. His object remains, – that of increasing the wisdom and happiness of mankind: but he has laid aside his wings, and added to the weight and purpose of his body: the spiritual part of him is invested with ordinary flesh and blood. In truth, for ordinary or immediate purposes, a great deal of Mr Shelley's poetry ought to have been written in prose. It consists of philosophical speculations, which required an introduction to the understandings of the community, and not merely, as he thought, a recommendation to their good will. The less philo-sophic he becomes, reverting to his own social feelings, as in some of the pathetic complaints before us; or appealing to the common ones of mankind upon matters immediately agitating them, as in the 'Ode to Naples'; or giving himself fairly up to the sports of fancy, as in the 'Witch of Atlas', or 'The Translations from Goethe and Homer'; the more he delights and takes with him, those who did not know whether to argue, or to feel, in

103

some of his larger works. The common reader is baffled with the perplexing mixture of passion and calmness; of the severest reasoning, and the wildest fiction; of the most startling appearances of dissent, and the most conventional calls upon sympathy. But in all his writings there is a wonderful sustained sensibility, and a language lofty and fit for it. He has the art of using the stateliest words and the most learned idioms, without incurring the charge of pedantry; so that passages of more splendid and sonorous writing are not to be selected from any writer, since the time of Milton: and yet when he descends from his ideal worlds, and comes home to us in our humbler bowers, and our yearnings after love and affection, he attunes the most natural feelings to a style so proportionate, and withal to a modulation so truly musical, that there is nothing to surpass it in the lyrics of Beaumont and Fletcher.

Lord Byron and His Contemporaries
1828

from Mr Keats

Mr Keats, when he died, had just completed his four-and-twentieth year. He was under the middle height; and his lower limbs were small in comparison with the upper, but neat and well-turned. His shoulders were very broad for his size: he had a face, in which energy and sensibility were remarkably mixed up, an eager power checked and made patient by ill-health. Every feature was at once strongly cut, and delicately alive. If there was any faulty expression, it was in the mouth, which was not without something of a character of pugnacity. The face was rather long than otherwise; the upper lip projected a little over the under; the chin was bold, the cheeks sunken; the eyes mellow and glowing; large, dark and sensitive. At the recital of a noble action, or a beautiful thought, they would suffuse with tears, and his mouth trembled.

In this, there was ill-health as well as imagination, for he did not like these betrayals of emotion; and he had great personal as well as moral courage. His hair, of a brown colour, was fine, and hung in natural ringlets. The head was a puzzle for the phrenologists, being remarkably small in the skull; a singularity which he had in common with Lord Byron and Mr Shelley, none of whose hats I could get on. Mr Keats was sensible of the disproportion above noticed, between his upper and lower extremities; and he would look at his hand, which was faded, and swollen in the veins, and say it was the hand of a man of fifty. He was a seven months' child: his mother, who was a lively woman, passionately fond of amusement, is supposed to have hastened her death by too great an inattention to hours and seasons. Perhaps she hastened that of her son.

Mr Keats's origin was of the humblest description; he was born October 29, 1796, at a livery-stables in Moorfields, of which his grandfather was the proprietor. I am very incurious, and did not know this till the other day. He never spoke of it, perhaps out of a personal soreness which the world had exasperated. After receiving the rudiments of a classical education at Mr Clarke's school at Enfield, he was bound apprentice to Mr Hammond, a surgeon, in Church-street, Edmonton; and his enemies having made a jest even of this, he did not like to be reminded of it; at once disdaining them for their meanness, and himself for being sick enough to be moved by them. Mr Clarke, junior, his schoolmaster's son, a reader of genuine discernment, had encouraged with great warmth the genius that he saw in the young poet; and it was to Mr Clarke I was indebted for my acquaintance with him. I shall never forget the impression made upon me by the exuberant specimens of genuine though young poetry that were laid before me, and the promise of which was seconded by the fine fervid countenance of the writer. We became intimate on the spot, and I found the young poet's heart as warm as his imagination. We read and walked together, and used to write verses of an evening upon a given subject. No imaginative pleasure was left unnoticed by us, or unenjoyed; from the recollection of the

105

bards and patriots of old, to the luxury of a summer rain at our window, or the clicking of the coal in winter-time. . . .

. . . When 'Endymion' was published, he was living at Hampstead with his friend Mr Charles Brown, who attended him most affectionately through a severe illness, and with whom, to their great mutual enjoyment, he had taken a journey into Scotland. The lakes and mountains of the North delighted him exceedingly. He beheld them with an epic eye. Afterwards, he went into the South, and luxuriated in the Isle of Wight. On Mr Brown's leaving England a second time, to visit the same quarter, Mr Keats, who was too ill to accompany him, came to reside with me, when his last and best volume of poems appeared, containing *Lamia*, *Isabella*, the *Eve of St Agnes*, and the noble fragment of *Hyperion*. I remember Charles Lamb's delight and admiration on reading this work; how pleased he was with the designation of Mercury as 'the star of Lethe' (rising, as it were, and glittering, as he came upon that pale region); with the fine daring anticipation in that passage of the second poem, –

> So the two brothers and *their murdered man*
> Rode past fair Florence;

and with the description, at once delicate and gorgeous, of Agnes praying beneath the painted window. This last (which should be called, *par excellence*, the Prayer at the Painted Window) has been often quoted; but for the benefit of those who are not yet acquainted with the author's genius, farther than by means of these pages, I cannot resist repeating it. It throws a light upon one's book.

> A casement high and triple-arch'd there was,
> All garlanded with carven imag'ries
> Of fruits, and flowers, and bunches of knot-grass,
> And diamonded with panes of quaint device,
> Innumerable of stains and splendid dyes,
> As are the tiger-moth's deep-damask'd wings;
> And in the midst, 'mong thousand heraldries,
> And twilight saints, and dim emblazonings,
> A shielded scutcheon blush'd with blood of queens and kings.

Full on this casement shone the wintry moon,
And threw warm gules on Madeline's fair breast,
As down she knelt for heaven's grace and boon;
Rose bloom fell on her hands, together press'd,
And on her silver cross soft amethyst,
And on her hair a glory, like a saint:
She seem'd a splendid angel, newly dress'd,
Save wings, for heaven.

The whole volume is worthy of this passage. Mr Keats is no
half-painter, who has only distinct ideas occasionally, and fills
up the rest with commonplaces. He feels all as he goes. In his
best pieces, every bit is precious; and he knew it, and laid it on
as carefully as Titian or Giorgione. Take a few more samples.

LOVERS

Parting they seem'd to tread upon the air,
Twin roses by the zephyr blown apart,
Only to meet again more close, and share
The inward fragrance of each other's heart.

BEES

Bees, the little almsmen of spring bowers.

A DELICATE SUPPER

And still she slept an azure-lidded sleep
In blanched linen, smooth and lavender'd,
While he from forth the closet brought a heap
Of candied apple, quince, and plum, and gourd;
With jellies soother than the creamy curd,
And lucent syrops, tint with cinnamon;
Manna and dates, in argosy transferr'd
From Fez; and spiced dainties, every one,
From silken Samarcand to cedar'd Lebanon.

These are stanzas, for which Persian kings would fill a poet's mouth with gold. I remember Mr Keats reading these lines to me with great relish and particularity, conscious of what he had set forth. The melody is as sweet as the subject, especially at 'Lucent syrops tinct with cinnamon', and the conclusion. Mr Wordsworth would say that the vowels were not varied enough; but Mr Keats knew where his vowels were *not* to be varied. On the occasion above alluded to, Mr Wordsworth found fault with the repetition of the concluding sound of the participles in Shakspeare's line about bees: 'The *singing* masons *building* roofs of gold'. This, he said, was a line which Milton would never have written. Mr Keats thought, on the other hand, that the repetition was in harmony with the continued note of the singers, and that Shakspeare's negligence (if negligence it was) had instinctively felt the thing in the best manner. The assertion about Milton startles one, considering the tendency of that great poet to subject his nature to art; yet I have dipped, while writing this, into *Paradise Lost*, and at the second chance have lit on the following:

> The gray
> Dawn, and the Pleiades before him danced,
> Shedding sweet influence. Less bright the moon,
> But opposite, *in levelled west, was set*
> His mirrour, with full force borrowing her light.

The repetition of the *e* in the fourth line is an extreme case in point, being monotonous to express one-ness and evenness. Milton would have relished the supper which his young successor, like a page for him, has set forth. It was Mr Keats who observed to me, that Milton, in various parts of his writings, has shown himself a bit of an epicure, and loves to talk of good eating. That he was choice in his food, and set store by a good cook, there is curious evidence to be found in the proving of his Will; by which it appears, that dining one day 'in the kitchen', he complimented Mrs Milton, by the appropriate title of 'Betty', on the dish she had set before him; adding, as if he could not pay her too well for it, 'Thou knowest I have left thee all'. Henceforth let a kitchen be illustrious, should a gentleman choose to take a cutlet in it. But houses and their customs were different in those days. . . .

It was Lord Byron, at that time living in Italy, drinking its wine, and basking in its sunshine, who asked me what was the meaning of a beaker 'full of the warm South'.[1] It was not the word beaker that puzzled him. College had made him intimate enough with that. But the sort of poetry in which he excelled, was not accustomed to these poetical concentrations. At the moment also, he was willing to find fault, and did not wish to discern an excellence different from his own. When I told him, that Mr Keats admired his *Don Juan*, he expressed both surprise and pleasure, and afterwards mentioned him with respect in a canto of it. He could not resist, however, making undue mention of one of the causes that affected his health. A good rhyme about *particle* and *article* was not to be given up. I told him he was mistaken in attributing Mr Keats's death to the critics, though they had perhaps hastened, and certainly embittered it; and he promised to alter the passage: but a joke and a rhyme together! Those Italian shrugs of the shoulders, which I hope will never be imported among us, are at once a lamentation and an excuse for every thing; and I cannot help using one here. At all events, I have kept my promise, to make the erratum myself in case it did not appear.

Mr Keats had felt that his disease was mortal for two or three years before he died. He had a constitutional tendency to consumption; a close attendance to the death-bed of a beloved brother, when he ought to have been nursing himself in bed, gave it a blow which he felt for months; and meanwhile the rascally critics came up, and roused an indignation in him, both against them and himself, which he could ill afford to endure. All this trouble was secretly aggravated by a very tender circumstance, which I can but allude to thus publicly, and which naturally subjected one of the warmest hearts and imaginations that ever existed, to all the pangs, that doubt, succeeded by delight, and delight, succeeded by hopelessness in this world, could inflict. Seeing him once change countenance in a manner more alarming than usual, as he stood silently eyeing the country out of window, I pressed him to let me know how he felt, in order that he might enable me to do what I could for him: upon which he said, that his feelings were almost more than he could bear, and that he feared for his senses. I proposed that we should take a coach, and ride about the country together, to vary, if possible, the immediate impression, which was sometimes all that was formidable, and would come to nothing. He acquiesced, and was restored to himself. It was nevertheless on the same day, sitting on the bench in Well Walk, at Hampstead, nearest the heath, that he told me, with unaccustomed tears in his eyes, that 'his heart was breaking.' A doubt, however, was upon him at the time, which he afterwards had reason to know was groundless; and during his residence at the last house that he occupied before he went abroad, he was at times more than tranquil. At length, he was persuaded by his friends to try the milder climate of Italy; and he thought it better for others as well as himself that he should go. He was accompanied by Mr Severn, a young artist of great promise, who has since been well known as the principal English student at Rome, and who possessed all that could recommend him for a companion, – old acquaintanceship, great animal spirits, active tenderness, and a mind capable of appreciating that of the poet. They went first to Naples, and afterwards to Rome; where, on the 27th of December, 1820,[2] our author died in the arms of his friend, completely worn out, and longing for the release. He suffered so much in his lingering, that he used to watch the countenance of the physician for the favourable and fatal sentence, and express his regret when he found it delayed. Yet no impatience escaped him. He was manly and gentle to the last, and grateful for all services. A little before he died, he said that he 'felt the daisies growing over him'. But he made a still more touching remark respecting his epitaph. 'If any,' he said, 'were put over him, he wished it to consist of nothing but these words: "Here lies one, whose name was writ in water"' – so little did he think of the more than promise he had given; – of the fine and lasting things he had added to the stock of poetry. The physicians expressed their astonishment that he had held out so long, the lungs turning out, on inspection, to have been almost obliterated. They said he must have lived upon the mere strength of the spirit within him. He was interred in the English burying-ground at Rome, near the monument of Caius Cestius, where his friend and poetical mourner, Mr Shelley, was soon to join him.

So much for the mortal life of as true a man of genius as these latter times have seen; one of those who are too genuine and too original to be properly appreciated at first, but whose time for applause will infallibly arrive with the many, and has already begun in all poetical quarters. I venture to prophesy, as I have done elsewhere, that Mr Keats will be known hereafter in English literature, emphatically, as *the Young Poet*; and that his volumes will be the sure companions, in field and grove, of all those who know what a luxury it is to hasten, with a favourite volume against one's heart, out of the strife of commonplaces into the haven of solitude and imagination.

Lord Byron and His Contemporaries
1828

Adonais

Since I left London, Mr Shelley's *Adonais, or Elegy on the Death of Mr Keats*, has, I find, made its appearance. I have not seen the London edition; but I have an Italian one printed at Pisa, with which I must content myself at present. The other was to have had notes. It is not a poem calculated to be popular, any more than the *Prometheus Unbound*; it is of too abstract and subtle a nature for that purpose; but it will delight the few, to whom Mr Shelley is accustomed to address himself. Spenser would be pleased with it if he were living. A mere town reader and a Quarterly Reviewer will find it *caviare*. *Adonais*, in short, is such an elegy as poet might be expected to write upon poet. The author has had before him his recollections of Lycidas, of Moschus and

111

Bion, and of the doctrines of Plato; and in the stanza of the most poetical of poets, Spenser, has brought his own genius, in all its etherial beauty, to lead a pomp of Loves, Graces, and Intelligences, in honour of the departed.

Nor is the Elegy to be considered less sincere, because it is full of poetical abstractions. Dr Johnson would have us believe that *Lycidas* is not 'the effusion of real passion'. – 'Passion', says he, in his usual conclusive tone, (as if the force of critic could no further go) 'plucks no berries from the myrtle and ivy; nor calls upon Arethuse and Mincius, nor tells of rough Satyrs and Fauns with cloven heel. Where there is leisure for fiction, there is little grief.' This is only a more genteel common-place, brought in to put down a vulgar one. Dr Johnson, like most critics, had no imagination; and because he found nothing natural to his own impulses in the associations of poetry, and saw them so often abused by the practice of versifiers inferior to himself, he was willing to conclude, that on natural occasions they were always improper. But a poet's world is as real to him as the more palpable one to people in general. He spends his time in it as truly as Dr Johnson did his in Fleet Street or at the club. Milton felt that the happiest hours he had passed with his friend had been passed in the regions of poetry. He had been accustomed to be transported with him 'beyond the visible diurnal sphere' of his fire-side and supper-table, things which he could record nevertheless with a due relish. (See the *Epitaphium Damonis*.) The next step was to fancy himself again among them, missing the dear companions of his walks; and then it is that the rivers murmur complainingly, and the flowers hang their heads, – which to a truly poetical habit of mind, though to no other, they may literally be said to do, because such is the aspect which they present to an afflicted imagination. 'I see nothing in the world but melancholy', is a common phrase with persons who are suffering under a great loss. With ordinary minds in this condition the phrase implies a vague feeling, but still an actual one. The poet, as in other instances, gives it a life and particularity. The practice has doubtless been abused; so much so, that even some imaginative minds may find it difficult at first to fall in with it, however beautifully managed. But the very abuse shews that it is founded in a principle in nature. And a great deal depends upon the character of the poet. What is mere frigidity and affectation in common magazine rhymers, or men of wit and fashion about town, becomes another thing in minds accustomed to live in the sphere I spoke of. It was as unreasonable in Dr Johnson to sneer at Milton's grief in *Lycidas*, as it was reasonable in him to laugh at Prior and Congreve for comparing Chloe to Venus and Diana, and *pastoralizing* about Queen Mary. Neither the turn of their genius, nor their habits of life, included this sort of ground. We feel that Prior should have stuck to his tuckers and boddices, and Congreve appeared in his proper Court-mourning.

Milton perhaps overdid the matter a little when he personified the poetical enjoyments of his friend and himself under the character of actual shepherds. Mr Shelley is the more natural in this respect, inasmuch as he is entirely abtract and imaginative, and recalls his lamented acquaintance to mind in no other shape than one strictly poetical. I say acquaintance, because such Mr Keats was; and it happens, singularly enough, that the few hours which he and Mr Shelley passed together were almost entirely of a poetical character. I recollect one evening in particular which they spent with the writer of these letters in composing verses on a given subject. But it is not as a mere acquaintance, however poetical, that Mr Shelley records him. It is as the intimate acquaintance of all lovely and lofty thoughts, as the nursling of the Muse, the hope of her coming days, the creator of additional Beauties and Intelligences for the adornment and inhabitation of the material world. The poet commences with calling upon Urania to weep for her favourite; and in a most beautiful stanza, the termination of which is in the depths of the human heart, informs us where he is lying. You are aware that Mr Keats died at Rome: –

> To that high Capital, where kingly Death
> Keeps his pale court in beauty and decay,
> He came; – and bought, with price of purest breath,

113

A grave among the eternal – Come away!
Haste, while the vault of blue Italian day
Is yet his fitting charnel-roof! while still
He lies, as if in dewy sleep he lay;
Awake him not! surely he takes his fill
Of deep and liquid rest, forgetful of all ill.

'The forms of things unseen', which Mr Keats' imagination had
turned into shape, – the 'airy nothings' to which it is the high
prerogative of the poet to give 'a local habitation and a name', are
then represented, in a most fanciful manner, as crowding about
his lips and body, and lamenting him who called them into being: –

And others came . . . Desires and Adorations,
Winged Persuasions and veiled Destinies,
Splendours, and glooms, and glimmering Incarnations
Of hopes and fears, and twilight Phantasies;
And Sorrow, with her family of sighs;
And Pleasure, blind with tears, led by the gleam
Of her own dying smile instead of eyes.
All he had loved, and moulded into thought,
From shape, and hue, and odour, and sweet sound,
Lamented Adonais.

A phrase in the first line of the following passage would make
an admirable motto for that part of the *Literary Pocket Book*, in
which the usual list of kings and other passing dominations are
superseded by a list of Eminent Men: –

And he is gathered to *the kings of thought*,
Who waged contention with their time's decay,
And of the past are all that cannot pass away.

The spot in which Mr Keats lies buried is thus finely pointed out.
The two similes at the close are among the happiest we recollect,
especially the second: –

Go thou to Rome, – at once the Paradise,
The grave, the city, and the wilderness;

And where its wrecks like shattered mountains rise,
And flowering weeds, and fragrant copses dress
The bones of Desolation's nakedness,
Pass, till the Spirit of the spot shall lead
Thy footsteps to a slope of green access,
Where, like an infant's smile, over the dead,
A light of laughing flowers along the grass is spread.

And gray walls moulder round, on which dull Time
Feeds, like slow fire upon a hoary brand.

In the course of the poem some living writers are introduced,
among whom Lord Byron is designated as

The Pilgrim of Eternity, whose fame
Over his living head like Heaven is bent
An early but enduring monument!

The poet of Ireland is called, with equal brevity and felicity, 'The
sweetest lyrist of her saddest wrong'.[1] And among 'others of less
note', is modestly put one, the description of whom is strikingly
calculated to excite a mixture of sympathy and admiration.[2] The
use of the Pagan mythology is supposed to have been worn out;
but in fact, they who say so, or are supposed to have worn it
out, never wore it at all. See to what a natural and noble purpose
a true scholar can turn it: –

He, as I guess,
Had gazed on Nature's naked loveliness,
Actæon-like, and now he fled astray
With feeble steps o'er the world's wilderness,
And his own thoughts, along that ragged way,
Pursued, like raging hounds, their father and their prey.

A pard-like Spirit, beautiful and swift –
A Love in desolation masked; – a Power
Girt round with weakness; – it can scarce uplift
The weight of the superincumbent hour;

115

It is a dying lamp, a falling shower,
A breaking billow; – even while we speak
Is it not broken? On the withering flower
The killing sun smiles brightly: on a cheek
The life can burn in blood, even while the heart may break.

> Ah! te meæ si partem animæ rapit
> Maturior vis! – –[3]

But the poet is here, I trust, as little of a prophet, as affection and
a beautiful climate, and the extraordinary and most vital energy
of his spirit, can make him. The singular termination of this
description, and the useful reflections it is calculated to excite, I
shall reserve for another subject in my next. But how is it, that
even that termination could not tempt the malignant commonplace of the Quarterly Reviewers to become blind to the obvious
beauty of this poem, and venture upon laying some of its noble
stanzas before their readers? How is it that in their late specimens
of Mr Shelley's powers they said nothing of the style and versification of the majestic tragedy of the *Cenci*, which would have
been equally intelligible to the lowest, and instructive to the highest, of their readers? How is it that they have not even hinted at
the existence of this *Elegy on the death of Mr Keats*, though immediately after the arrival of copies of it from Italy they thought proper
to give a pretended review of a poem which appeared to them
the least calculated for their readers' understandings? And
finally, how happens it, that Mr Gifford has never taken any
notice of Mr Keats' *last* publication, – the beautiful volume containing *Lamia*, the Story from Boccaccio, and that magnificent
fragment *Hyperion*?[4] Perhaps the following passage of the Elegy
will explain: –

> Our Adonais has drunk poison! – Oh,
> What deaf and viperous murderer could crown
> Life's early cup with such a draught of woe?
> The nameless worm would not itself disown:
> It felt, yet could escape the magic tone

116

Whose prelude held all envy, hate, and wrong,
But what was howling in one breast alone
Silent with expectation, of the song,
Whose master's hand is cold, whose silver lyre unstrung.

Live thou, whose infamy is not thy fame!
Live! fear no heavier chastisement from me,
Thou noteless blot on a remembered name!
But be thyself, and know thyself to be!
And ever at thy season be thou free
To spill the venom when thy fangs o'erflow:
Remorse and Self-Contempt shall cling to thee;
Hot Shame shall burn upon thy secret brow,
And like a beaten hound tremble thou shalt – as now.

This, one would think, would not have been 'unintelligible' to
the dullest *Quarterly* peruser, who had read the review of Mr
Keats' *Endymion*. Nor would the following perhaps have been
quite obscure: –

Nor let us weep that our delight is fled
Far from these carrion kites that scream below;
He wakes or sleeps with the enduring dead;
Thou canst not soar where he is sitting now.
Dust to the dust! but the pure spirit shall flow
Back to the burning fountain whence it came,
A portion of the Eternal, which must glow
Through time and change, unquenchably the same,
While thy cold embers choke the sordid hearth of shame.

However, if further explanation had been wanted, the Preface
to the Elegy furnishes it in abundance, which even the meanest
admirers of Mr Gifford could have no excuse for not understanding? Why then did he not quote this? Why could he not venture,
once in his life, to try and look a little fair and handsome; and
instead of making all sorts of misrepresentations of his opponents, lay before his readers something of what his opponents
say of him? He only ventures to allude, in convulsive fits and

117

starts, and then not by name, to the *Feast of the Poets*. He dare not even allude to Mr Hazlitt's epistolary dissection of him. And now he, or some worthy coadjutor for him, would pretend that he knows nothing of Mr Shelley's denouncement of him, but criticises his other works out of pure zeal for religion and morality! Oh these modern 'Scribes, Pharisees, and Hypocrites!' How exactly do they resemble their prototypes of old!

'It may well be said', observes Mr Shelley's Preface, 'that these wretched men know not what they do. They scatter their insults and their slanders without heed as to whether the poisoned shaft lights on a heart made callous by many blows, or one, like Keats's, composed of more penetrable stuff. One of their associates is, to my knowledge, a most base and unprincipled calumniator. As to "Endymion", was it a poem, whatever might be its defects, to be treated contemptuously by those who had celebrated with various degrees of complacency and panegyric, "Paris", and "Woman", and a "Syrian Tale", and Mrs Lefanu, and Mr Barrett, and Mr Howard Payne, and a long list of the illustrious obscure?[5] Are these the men, who in their venal good-nature, presumed to draw a parallel between the Rev. Mr Milman and Lord Byron?[6] What gnat did they strain at here, after having swallowed all those camels? Against what woman taken in adultery, dares the foremost of these literary prostitutes to cast his opprobrious stone? Miserable man! you, one of the meanest, have wantonly defaced one of the noblest specimens of the workmanship of God. Nor shall it be your excuse, that murderer as you are, you have spoken daggers but used none.'

Let us take the taste of the Gifford out of one's mouth with the remainder of the Preface, which is like a sweet nut after one with a worm in it.

'The circumstances of the closing scene of poor Keats's life were not made known to me until the Elegy was ready for the press. I am given to understand that the wound which his sensitive spirit had received from the criticism of "Endymion", was exasperated by the bitter sense of unrequited benefits; the poor fellow seems to have been hooted from the stage of life, no less

118

by those on whom he had wasted the promise of his genius, than those on whom he had lavished his fortune and his care. He was accompanied to Rome, and attended in his last illness by Mr Severn, a young artist of the highest promise, who, I have been informed, "almost risked his own life, and sacrificed every prospect to unwearied attendance upon his dying friend." Had I known these circumstances before the completion of my poem, I should have been tempted to add my feeble tribute of applause to the more solid recompense which the virtuous man finds in the recollection of his own motives. Mr Severn can dispense with a reward from "such stuff as dreams are made of". His conduct is a golden augury of the success of his future career – may the unextinguished Spirit of his illustrious friend animate the creations of his pencil, and plead against oblivion for his name!'

Amen! says one who knew the poet, and who knows the painter.

The Examiner
7 July 1822

Poems by Alfred Tennyson
2 vols., 1842

Only one of these volumes is entirely new. The first, as the author intimates in two successive dates at the beginning and middle of it, and a little more copious bit of information in four lines at the conclusion, is for the most part a collection of former volumes, and some of the poems in it have been 'considerably altered'. Others, he might have added, have been left out; and, retaining what he has, we do not see good reason for the omission: so that the present publication is neither an entire collection, nor a thoroughly satisfactory selection, which is a pity.

We state our objections first, that we may get rid of the unpleasant part of our task, and enjoy the subsequent approbation with more comfort; for, though reviewers are supposed to take a special delight in censure, and we ourselves must in candour confess that we know what it is to be tempted to go the way of all critical flesh, and how strong the desire in the young reviewer is to make the importance of the judgment-seat felt; but a little more Christian reflection made us discern the danger which our love of truth was undergoing, especially towards persons who differed with us in opinion; and, though we must never cease to find fault where truth demands it, and where the book is of importance enough to render fault-finding necessary (for wretched books may surely be left to their own natural death, without exciting a shabby desire to kill them), yet, so far from giving either into this once reigning bad habit of reviews, or into the other pick-thank extreme of indiscriminate praise, or following the still more common and servile practice of giving the greatest praise to none but authors in fashion, and being afraid of doing justice to others perhaps far superior, we shall make it our business to give as cheerful and even reverential eulogy to genius, in whatever quarter we find it, as we shall jealously guard that right and sincerity of objection which alone can render it thoroughly valuable. We would not give wholesale, indiscriminate laudation to Shakspeare himself, as long as human nature is what it is, and no man perfect. Neither, on the other hand, shall any reigning fashion induce us to take commonplace for invention, or the soothing of the languors of soft ears for a masculine versification.

We are compelled to say, then, in justice to the very respect which we entertain, and the more which we desire to entertain, for the genius of Mr Tennyson, that the above 'lettings out of the bag' of his dates and alterations, are a little too characteristic of a certain mixture of timidity and misgiving with his otherwise somewhat defying demands upon our assent to his figments and his *hyphens*, and that we have greater objections to a certain air of literary dandyism, or fine-gentlemanism, or fastidiousness, or whatever he may *not* be pleased to call it, which leads him to usher in his compositions with such exordiums as those to 'Morte d' Arthur', and 'Godiva'; in the former of which he gives us to understand that he should have burnt his poem but for the

120

'request of friends'; and, in the latter, that he 'shaped' it while he was waiting 'for the train at Coventry', and hanging on the bridge 'with grooms and porters'. Really this is little better than the rhyming fine-ladyism of Miss Seward,[1] who said that she used to translate an ode of Horace 'while her hair was curling'. And, if the 'grooms and porters' have any meaning beyond a superfluous bit of the graphic, not in keeping with his subject, it is a little worse, for why should not Mr Tennyson, in the universality of his poetry, be as content to be waiting on a bridge, among 'grooms and porters', as with any other assortment of his fellow-men? Doubtless he would disclaim any such want of philosophy; but this kind of mixed tone of contempt and nonchalance, or, at best, of fine-life phrases with better fellowship, looks a little instructive, and is, at all events, a little perilous. There is a drawl of Bond-street in it. We suspect that these poems of 'Morte d' Arthur' and 'Godiva' are among those which Mr Tennyson thinks his best, and is most anxious that others should regard as he does; and therefore it is that he would affect to make trifles of them. The reader's opinion is at once to be of great importance to him, and yet none at all. There is a boyishness in this which we shall be happy to see Mr Tennyson, who is no longer a boy, outgrow.

So of his hyphens and his dots, his *sëers*, *low-lieths*, and *Eleanoras*, and the intensifications of his prefix *a* – *aweary, amany, anear*; it is 'affectations, 'oman', as Sir Hugh says;[2] and a very unnecessary bad compliment both to his readers and himself, as if they did not know how to read, or could never enough see the merit of his quantities and qualities without the help of his lackadaisical particle. Upon a like principle we object to his excessive fondness for repeating a lyrical 'burthen'. His 'aweary, aweary', in the 'Moated Grange', may indeed help us to sympathise with the fatigue of the inhabitant; but four 'Orianas' to every stanza, in the ballad of that name, amounting to forty-four in all, burlesque all music and feeling, and become a parrot-cry instead of a melody. This, too, in a poem full of beauty!

We trust that in his next publication Mr Tennyson will show

121

that he has acquired energy enough to get rid of these mixtures of weakness with his strength. We do not wish him, merely because critics object to them, to leave out some of his second or third-best productions, as he seems to have done, and this, too, while retaining his most objectionable; we desire to see him once for all at ease both with his critics and himself, acknowledge what is juvenile or faulty, or rather perceive it without saying anything about the matter; and, whether he discountenances anything or nothing of what he has done, cease to combine misgiving with rashness, and airs of the drawing-room with the enlargement he really possesses, and give us a good, wholesome, satisfactory, and enduring quintessence of the best part of him. He has fancy, imagination, expression, thought, knowledge, and music, too – in short, all the materials of an admirable contemplative poet, and in some instances his success has been already great, and his name, we trust, will be lasting. But at present he still shows a little too much of the spoiled child. He is indolent, over-refining, is in danger of neutralizing his earnestness altogether by the scepticism of thought not too strong, but not strong enough to lead or combine, and he runs, or rather reposes, altogether upon feelings (not to speak it offensively) too sensual. His mind lives in an atmosphere heavy with perfumes. He grows lazy by the side of his Lincolnshire water-lilies; and, with a genius of his own sufficient for original and enduring purposes (at least we hope so), subjects himself to the charge of helping it too much with the poets gone before him, from Homer to Wordsworth, and to Shelley and Keats. But we will touch upon most of the poems in their order, and thus best show what we mean. The beautiful passages that we shall have to quote in eulogy will luckily far more than repay the reader and ourselves for any unpleasant necessity of finding fault.

'Claribel', who 'low-lieth' where the 'beetle *boometh*' (not a good word), and the 'wild bee hummeth', and the 'lint-white swelleth', and the 'mavis dwelleth', *et cetera, et cetera*, is rather a series of descriptive items in obsolete language than a dirge in earnest.

'Lilian' is as light and pretty as its subject; but

> Till the lightning laughters dimple
> The baby roses in her cheeks,

is an instance of that injudicious crowding of images which sometimes results from Mr Tennyson's desire to impress upon us the abundance of his thoughts.

The style of 'Isabel' reminds us both of Wordsworth's solemnity and Shelley's Grecisms and penultimate accents. It is a panegyric of chastity in that ultra-super-exalting spirit of Beaumont and Fletcher, which renders the sincerity of it suspicious; and the conclusion unluckily corroborates the impression by informing us that 'the world hath not such another', for a 'finished, chastened purity', as this lady! This is awkward for the sex in general, and for their gratitude to the poet. The expression '*blanched* tablets of the heart', will not do at all after its beautiful original in the old poet, 'the *red-leaved* tablets of the heart'. There is a charming verisimilitude and warmth of feeling in the latter image, full of grace and cordiality.

'Mariana', in the 'Moated Grange', brings us at once into the thick of the real beauties of the author; and, as we have not noticed him in this publication before, and wish our article to give as thorough an idea of his genius as it can, we will quote the whole of it, though at the hazard of the reader's having seen it years ago. The loose, rusty nails on the garden wall, the 'glooming flats', the low of the oxen coming from the dark fens, the blue fly singing in the pane, and the mouse shrieking behind the mouldering wainscot, are part of a heap of images all painted from nature, and true to the feeling of the subject. . . .

Mr Tennyson seems to have felt that these descriptions, beautiful as they were, were rather native than foreign; and he has accordingly given us a 'Mariana in the South'; which, though more Catholic in one sense is less so in another; and though not without its truth too, and beauty, must undergo the fate of all sequels, in being considered very inferior to its prototype.

'Madeline' is held forth to us a lady, who 'smiling frowning evermore', is considered 'perfect in love' [*sic*: love-lore]. 'Delicious

123

spites and darling angers' are here; things such as Tasso took delight in praising; and as long as they only amused him, they were very well; but when he came to take a deeper interest, adieu to the lovingness of the lady and to his own happiness. So with this ever frowning and smiling coquette of Mr Tennyson's, who fixes a smile at him if he offers to go, and then 'blushes angerly' if he offers to kiss the tips of her fingers. We confess we have no faith in the lady's knowledge of love at all, nor any vast deal in the loveability of Mr Tennyson's ladies in general. They remind us too much of the fine young ladies in souvenirs and beauty-books, with rapturous eyes, dark locks and tresses, and all that – ready made to conquer between the meretricious and the moral – between a boarding-school education, and prudential, and in truth cold contradictions to it. He has a whole seraglio of them. The list would make a song of itself. There is Mariana, Eleonora, Oriana, Fatima, Dora, Margaret, Olivia, Rose, Emilia, Claribel, Isabel, Adeline, Madeline, Lady Clara, and Lady Flora. Poets are bound to be admirers of the fair sex; but Mr Tennyson talks as if he really loved most of these ladies, while it is pretty clear that his admiration is of a very ordinary sort, and that he makes the poor creatures pegs to hang characters upon; for which we are not surprised that they seldom appear to return his passion. We think him more ingenious than happy in these portraitures. There is sometimes a good deal of observation in them, and metaphys-ical acuteness; but it is too ostentatiously shown, often in num-bers affectedly musical; and he makes them so very conscious, or fastidious, or stately, or in some way or other almost always puts some such unpleasant contradiction to their loveability in the midst of their exuberant airs and graces, that they end in impressing us as a sort of poetical milliners, or artificial idealisms full dressed. And how can he condescend to write such fantastic nothings, pretending to be intense somethings, as the following:[3]

> Lovest thou the doleful wind
> When thou gazest at the skies?
> Doth the low-tongued Orient

Wander from the side of the morn,
Dripping with Sabæan spice
On thy pillow, lowly bent
With melodious airs lovelorn,
Breathing light against thy face,
While his locks *a-dropping* twined,
Round thy neck in subtle ring
Make a carcanet of rays,
(The meaning?)
And ye talk together still,
In the language wherewith spring
Letters cowslips on the hill?
Hence that look and smile of thine,
Spiritual Adeline!

We have read of lettered hyacinths in Theocritus (alluding to the story in the Mythology), and of 'shuttles of the morn', in a very different poet, one Mr Merry, hight Della Crusca,[4] who described them as 'weaving an airy lay upon a cobwebbed thorn'; and we must say that in such verses as these, Mr Tennyson reminds us far more of the gossamer fancies of that gentleman, than of his worthier and more kindred associate....

... There has been a reaction of late years in favour both of thought and feeling, and a very salutary reaction it is, against the unthinking commonplace that prevailed at the beginning of the century; but, with the usual tendency of revolutions, it has gone to an extreme, and young poets are in danger of exchanging one set of impertinences, that is to say, irrelevancies, for another. They *think* they must *think* at any rate, and be in an incessant state of exuberant remark and imagery, in order to shew what is in them. But real abundance is not under the necessity of taking those violent measures to prove itself. Everything even said well is not said fitly. The real feeling is apt to become smothered in the false; thought takes its place, and that alone is perilous; genuine powers prematurely exhibit themselves, taking pains to shew they have come to their full growth, with airs of universality, and profundity, and final judgments; till at last they are in danger of meeting with a very awkward extreme, and, instead of hitting the real points of their subject, whirl their giddy heads round towards the gentle outer-pole of the heroes of the *Dunciad*,

Who wrote *about* it, goddess, and *about* it.[5]

Now, one thing said with thorough truth, and to the purpose, is worth millions of half-apposite fancies, and similes, and collateralities, which do but end, as Ovid calls it, in a poverty-stricken abundance – *inops copia*,[6] and leave every poem of necessity unfinished: for where so many things are said *about* things, why not say more? or where is to be the end of them? Writers of this kind are apt to look with scorn on such poets as Gray and Collins, much more on Pope and the other poets of the French school. We ourselves are adherents to poetry in all its grades, and love the miniatures of Pope, notwithstanding our far greater love and delight in Spenser and Shakspeare, and our admiration of all the genuine intermediate good stuff, whether of thought or feeling, or both, in Beaumont and Fletcher, and Webster, and Marlowe, and Donne, and Daniel, and Drayton; but we cannot blind ourselves to the fact that completeness – judgment, a thing select – and passion, a thing with 'no nonsense' – and imagination, not to be confounded with thoughts and fancies, any more than quantity is quality, or profession performance. And the danger to these gentlemen is that the Grays and Collinses, and even that of the simply natural in Goldsmith, will survive them, and see most of them even speedily perish, unless they 'change their hand and check their pride', simply because those writers are consistent with the truth that is in them, and are not always provoking and disappointing the degree of expectation which they have undertaken to raise.

Mr Tennyson is at present a kind of philosophical Keats, without the later judgment of that extraordinary genius, and of a turn of mind less naturally and thoroughly given to poetry, in its essence. But there can be no doubt that he is a genuine poet too in his degree (a sacred name – pray let him know how to value it, and be at his ease with it): and there is a class of poetry in which we think he may obtain for himself a name, perhaps as great in its way as that of the other, and one of an independent sort, and that is in a mixture of thought and feeling, more abundant in the former respect than Keats, and more pleasurable and luxuriant in the latter than Wordsworth. We have already characterized, at the beginning of our article, his poetical merits as well as defects, and surely out of all these he might produce another volume which, if less in bulk than the two before us, would have a far greater real abundance. His poems of 'Mariana', and 'A Character', and the 'Merman' and 'Mermaid', and 'Oriana' (in spite of its burden), and the 'Miller's Daughter', and 'Simeon Stylites', and the 'Two Voices', are almost all written in a style as clear and compact as the fancy and imagination are poetical, and the thinking profound; and we hope to see the day when Mr Moxon will oblige us with a volume including these, and containing new ones nothing inferior to the old.

Such is the position, in the opinion of poets and lovers of genuine poetry (the opinion of critics, and of the public, may not as yet be quite in accordance with the former), which Mr Tennyson has attained after having been before the world during ten or twelve years. With the first class his genius was at once recognized – with the critics and the public it has, as usual, been matter of slow progress and much contest; but we think that, on the whole, he has little reason to be dissatisfied, and no reason at all, when we consider the ill treatment and tardy admission of the claims of Shelley, of Keats, and of Wordsworth.

Ainsworth's Magazine
1842

Rules for the Conduct of Newspaper Editors with Respect to Politics and News

One cannot help smiling to think of the numberless folios which have been written on the art of politics. Mankind really seem to have imagined, that it was extremely difficult in the precept as well as practice; and from Confucius to Plato, from Plato to Justinian, from Justinian to Machiavel, from Machiavel to Montesquieu, a thousand extravagant praises have been bestowed upon political scribblers. I cannot discover, for the life of me, what peculiar talent could have been found in such writers. Some of them may be allowed to possess a shade of imagination, but what are called your sound politicians must evidently be very inferior men, for they confess they have nothing to do with either enthusiasm or fancy; and what is genius without these qualities? Nay, they absolutely acknowledge that they estimate little but experience and mere matter of fact. I only wish, that the newspaper politicians were confined to matter of fact for a few months, and we should soon see what would be the fate of political composition.

It has been said by philosophers, that the end of instruction is to elevate man to wisdom; but I think that he is a much nobler teacher who brings down wisdom to man. It would be much happier for the mind if it could be wise without exertion, and I really cannot see much art in this boasted ascension to knowledge. It is very well to go up the stairs of St Paul's to examine the cross, but it would certainly be much better if one could whistle the cross down. For this reason, I have endeavoured to simplify the rules of newspaper politics, and instead of making my readers toil up a ladder, like Gulliver, to read gigantic folios, have reduced this sublime science to the most inexcursive and unambitious comprehension.

1. OF POLITICAL ATTACHMENTS

You must absolutely be a party-man, or you are neither a true editor nor a true patriot. Patriotism consists in a love of one's country, and a love of one's country is certainly not a love of it considered in its earthly qualities, not a love of muddy Brentford or calcareous Margate, but an attachment to the best men in the country. Now the best citizen is he who would do most good to his fellow-citizens, and as every man must judge for himself, the best statesman is he who offers you the best place. It becomes you, therefore, to support him on every occasion, and particularly when he is wrong; for who would expose the errors of his friend?

2. OF EDITORSHIP CONSIDERED ABSTRACTEDLY FROM PROPRIETORSHIP

If you are proprietor as well as editor of your paper, you have the truly English freedom of saying what you please for your patron: but if you are editor only, it becomes you to say every thing which the proprietors may dictate, and nothing to which they may object. This restriction may appear hard, but in difficult times you must be hardened to meet difficulties; you are the servant of the proprietors, and inclination must be sacrificed to duty. What is called spirit will not pay your bills. The man who digs for money must of necessity stoop very low to find it.

3. OF POLITICAL CONTROVERSY

It is manifest, that every man who differs with your favourite leader must be miserably defective either in his head or his heart, but most likely in both. This is so self-evident, that it requires no argument. As to those insipid hypocrites, who pretend to be of no party, avoid them as so many newspaper outlaws, who are cut off from the social bustle of dispute. A writer of no party must be of no feeling, or at any rate a gross libeller on the public, for he must either have no capability of attachment or he must plainly tell the public, that there is not one of all their favourites who is worthy of entire co-operation. Give therefore no quarter to any writer of any party or of no party: if you wish to produce a revolution in political thinking, you must be strenuous and ardent. The principle of the lever has nothing to do with moving the human mind. You must oppose ponderousness to weight and rage to violence. The heaviness of some papers and the fury of others will afford you excellent examples. But above all, never lay yourself open to what is called conviction: you might as well open your waistcoat to receive a knock-down blow. A man will shut his eyes to an ugly sight, and I should be glad to know why he may not shut them to an uncomfortable argument. Give all the blows you can and receive none: newspaper controversy is a true battle; the soldiers have no business to argue about reason, they must only do all the mischief possible. In fact a playful moderation in politics is just as absurd as a remonstrative whisper to a mob. I have heard of a lad who nibbed one of his long nails and wrote with it, and as he most probably wrote very badly, I dare say that from this circumstance a bad penman is said to write a fist. Now you must write with your fist, that is, you must always argue by personal attack. Would you attempt to conquer a prize-fighter by chucking him playfully under the chin? Then how would you conquer the *Belchers* and *Game Chickens* of newspaper controversy but by opposing to them the *Gulleys* and the *Gregsons*! Your sentences must be so many metaphorical bruises; if you cannot reach your adversary's head, aim directly at his heart, and in the intervals of the battle amuse yourself by calling him names. If a man could save his country by being vulgar, who would be a gentleman? The greatest reformers, such as Luther and Calvin, have shewn a very proper contempt for mere refinement. If Luther, in the gaiety of his ardour, calls Calvin a *fool* and an *ass*, Calvin, in the consistency of his argument, calls Luther a *hog, beast, wretch, madman*, and *devil*. I would recommend to you three exquisite sentences of the Genevese Doctor as a specimen of warrantable energy: he says to Luther, after a few convincing arguments, 'Do you mind me, you dolt? Do you hear what I say, you madman? Do you listen to that, you great beast?'* I will be judged by any body, whether, with the exception of a little want of christian spirit, these figures of speech are not the exact models of a spirited disputation.

* This is quoted from memory, but it is not the smallest exaggeration.

4. OF INVENTION IN NEWS

The art of newspaper politics certainly cannot rank among the polite arts, but nevertheless it requires almost as much fancy as poetry or painting. This is peculiarly apparent in the periodical accounts of battles. A skilful editor shall describe heroes, dispose of armies, and dispense victories and defeats with all the fire and invention of Homer. If your favourite statesman is in office, it is your business to announce nothing but victories; if he is out, conquest must vanish with him. While you are in opposition, you must lament the total want of foresight in Ministers, their useless expeditions and senseless expenditures, and you must praise the French Emperor: while you are ministerial, you must insist and swear, not forgetting to stake the credit of your paper, that the country is in the best of all exquisite situations, that the expeditions will settle the balance of the world, that the opposition is an infamous faction, and that Napoleon is a Corsican tyrant and usurper. If the enemy gains a decided victory, you will swear that the two armies parted, but certainly with an advantage on our side: if the two armies really part, you have nothing to do but gain a victory. At the beginning of a campaign however you must always gain victories. It is an indispensable rule. If you hear, for instance, that the French and Russians are about to meet, be certain that the French are defeated with great slaughter, and announce the intelligence in capitals worthy of the occasion, as thus, DEFEAT AND SURRENDER OF THE WHOLE OF THE GRAND FRENCH ARMY. I need not tell you to use a smaller type when you are in opposition, that is, provided you are simple enough to say any thing to the credit of Ministers. At such a season, pomp is unsuitable both to a manly grief and to a proper enjoyment of victory. If you should be so bashful as to feel awkward, when the victories you have announced for the Ministry prove to be defeats, you have an excellent answer to all complaints in the reply of that admirable statesman Stratocles, who arrived at Athens from a naval defeat, put a chaplet on his head, and made all the citizens feast and sacrifice in honour of the

131

glorious victory; and when the shattered fleet arrived two days after, and the people called upon him to answer for his imposture, cried out, 'Why you will not quarrel with me for having given you two days of jollity?' Plutarch calls this impudence; but it is evident, that he knew as little of true policy, as our newspaper politicians know of him.

5THLY AND LASTLY, OF EDITORIAL SENSIBILITY, OR OF BEING HAPPY TO HEAR AND SORRY TO STATE

Great geniuses are always men of great feeling. If you keep all your frowns and your terrors for your enemies and rivals, you must preserve all your smiles and tears for the interesting occurrences of the fashionable world. Home news is the most pathetic thing in the world, and an Editor never appears to such advantage as when, like Homer's *Andromache*, he smiles and weeps at one instant. Thus if in one paragraph you exclaim with vivacity 'We are happy to hear that the Duke of Queensbury has recovered from his fit of the gout' – in the next you will probably observe with pathos 'We are sorry to state that serious apprehensions are entertained of the life of the illustrious Officer, who after having dined very heartily on Thursday last, slipped down upon the ice as he was passing through King's place.' Again, if you very naturally rub your hands in another paragraph, and cry out 'We are sincerely happy to hear that the Marchioness of S – – was *not* thrown from her horse in the act of spurring the animal,' you will have every reason to shake your heads in the next and exclaim 'We are sincerely sorry to state that the Right Hon. Lord B. was thrown out of his curricle and terribly bruised. His legs were found to be quite black.'

Thus then with talents for disputation, talents for fiction, and talents for weeping and smiling, no Editor need be afraid of being quite poor, provided he does not become an honest man.

The Examiner
6 March 1808

Distressed Seamen and the
Distress of the Poor in General

We write in behalf of this gallant and suffering body of men,
while the fierce winds, which they have so often battled with,
are roaring about our ears. Those winds, which in their muttering
intervals seem to be scorning human weakness, and then in their
wilder contempt to come rushing over our petty affectations of
pride and power, – what do *they* say to our rulers respecting the
darers of storms and waves? They seem to say, – We sweep the
ocean now as we will; the gallantest spirits among you are wanted
no longer to contend with us, and you neglect them; they who
dared us at our height, and who ran the race of the elements
with us over the tops of the waters, you now suffer to be shrunk
up with poverty and nakedness, and to be forced to hide from
us under bulks and penthouses! Do *you* pretend to be the master-
spirits of the world! We roll over your heartless nonsense with
disdain.

The conduct of Government indeed on occasions of this kind
is most extraordinary. Whenever sailors are wanted during a war,
we hear of nothing but their gallantry and infinite services; – 'the
gallant tars', the 'hearts of oak', the lions in battle and lambs
afterwards, the conquerors but to save, the heroes of 'our wooden
walls', the invincible maintainers of the British flag, the sweepers
of the seas, England's impregnable bulwarks, – what should we
do without them? – and accordingly when we cannot do without
them, we praise and flatter them to the skies; their virtues are
every thing that is generous and fine-hearted; their defects are
stuffed out into virtues; they are the representatives and epitomes
of all that is truly English; they sail off among shouts and hurras,
they meet the enemy, plunge into all the chaos of battle, get
lopped, maimed, splintered, burnt, bruised, battered, blown up,
drenched in water and in blood; return with thinned numbers,
with tattered flags, and with wounds; and there is an illumina-
tion. The Boroughmongers have dinners together; some Officers
get promoted, if they have interest; others commence a life of

half-pay and tattered memorials; the Government papers talk of glory, safety, magnanimity, invincibility, proud day, and eternal gratitude; such of the 'gallant tars', as have 'had the luck to have their legs shot off', have a chance of getting into Greenwich Hospital; the rest, who have the merit only of courage and poverty, must congratulate themselves on having their legs to live upon; and a creature of the name of Croker begins speculating how he shall keep a war-salary in time of peace.[1]

Such has been the case, more or less, during our naval wars and the intervals. Whenever the necessity for battle comes again, then the trumpets and flatteries are revived, and we are to have eternal glory, and to shew eternal gratitude. When the necessity is over, the trumpets and flatteries are dumb, and we hear a vast deal about impostors. At last, the seas are absolutely swept clean of all our enemies; we say so, and boast of it; and shortly after, we hear that multitudes of Seamen are perishing in our streets. *Twice*, since the close of the war, has their condition been brought before Government; *twice* have others done what the Government ought to have done; and *twice* have the Government rather acquiesced in the proposal made for relieving them, than blushed for their previous neglect, and taken up the subject warmly. It was that active and meritorious person, the late Lord Mayor,[2] who first urged it to them, – who first urged them to cast a gracious eye towards hundreds of their own saviours. A ship, with some coyness, was granted for their accommodation, – one perhaps in which many of these saviours had fought and bled, and had their limbs torn asunder, that we might all enjoy ourselves safe and sound at home. What is better, they were relieved of their nakedness out of the naval stores; and for a time, people thought that the preservers of our homes had something like a bit of a home as well as ourselves. But somehow or other, this ship has disappeared; nobody can tell what has become of it; a grave and prudent Government Alderman says he cannot even venture to guess; and in the mean time, multitudes of shivering and starving sailors having again made their appearance, something must be done again by persons out of the pale of Government,

134

and again the Government is applied to. It answers, it will do what it can 'with propriety', a ship or two is granted as before, and hundreds of Seamen have already been relieved by persons, who have neither the means, nor the influence, nor the imperious duty upon them to interfere in such cases, which Government has.

Now, that these persons have so interfered, and that hundreds of the Seamen have been relieved in consequence, is a most excellent thing; but the public have a right to demand a most serious explanation from Government. Did the Admiralty and others mean them to do nothing at all, had others done nothing? It seems so. And how are they to account for their neglect, as it is? For our parts, we cannot, with all the ingenuity we can muster up, and really with all the sincerity we can add to it, present to our imagination one single excuse they can have to make. That they were not aware of the circumstances, they cannot possibly say; that it is not a case under their jurisdiction, the Sailors not being in actual service, they cannot with any decency say either, when we consider how they interfere with their press-warrants, and how they take cognizance of all things connected with the service that are at all to their advantage, though, now we think of it, we suspect that this will be their attempt at an excuse. That the country does not owe at least sufficient gratitude to Seamen to keep them from starving, the hardiest of them (we mean the hardiest-faced) will not venture to assert; and if the country owes thus much, which is the most decent medium through which it shall be paid? That they have no funds, is another thing impossible to allege; for where, as Lord Cochrane asked, are the Droits of Admiralty,[3] and to whom do those misused funds belong, if not to the Seamen who won them? They they have no money to *spare*, can still less, if possible, be alleged; for they have several rank sinecures among their lordly offices, the existence of which is a scandal at any time, much more in times like the present. And granting that even that were not the case, there is not a Lord or Secretary of the Admiralty who ought not to forego at least the most unnecessary part of his luxuries, when such objects as

135

these were brought before his attention. But *this*! Oh, *this* would be reckoned prodigiously romantic, that is to say, silly! We cannot but fancy Mr Croker chuckling over the idea! And yet these men and their masters are among the persons who call upon *us*, upon the rest of the world, for generosities and sacrifices of all sorts! They have succeeded, till lately, upon the strength of the world's being more generous and trusting than themselves; but cunning is not wisdom, though it may ape it for a time; and the world are so thoroughly disgusted and undeceived at last, that these generosities and sacrifices will not be found forthcoming much longer. And this is the time which the servants of the Borough-mongers select for disgusting the community with their conduct to one of the bravest part of it! the time which they select for reminding us of their former flatteries and uproarious congratu-lations, by looking cold upon their friends and saviours, and talking of doing what they can 'with *propriety*!' Oh, if these gent-lemen had *been fought* for, only as far as '*propriety*' went! If their respective natures and intentions had all been inquired into to see which of them could or could not have been kept safe and sound, and suffered to grow rich, with '*propriety*!' If their words, actions, possessions, or claims had all been made to undergo the test of '*propriety*!' Propriety means right of possession, what is proper or belonging to any one, *own*-ness; and by moral metaphor, it comes to mean decency, justice, what is becoming under such and such circumstances, what is due to this or that person, or set of persons, and may in moral as well as civil justice be called their own, whether all or in part. Now we should like to hear the inheritor of Lord Melville's fortune and titles, or Mr Croker who wanted to have so many salaries of widows in addi-tion to his own, discuss to us the particular use of the word on the present occasion. We know not the talents of his Lordship this way nor how far he could make the meaning and application of the term fall in with the Droits and the Sinecures; but with Mr Croker, who has read Shakspeare, propriety is doubtless – as it were – a sort of – as one should say – propriety; that is, if one is very hard pushed, and obliged to face the matter out, propriety is letting hundreds of human beings, who have been the saviours of us, huddle together under pent-houses, cold, hungry, and sick, – and adding to one's own salary, already undeserved, in order that we may be able to give dinners to our great friends the Boroughmongers.

The Examiner
18 January 1818

Cause of the Inferiority of Parliament to the Demands of the Present Age

What renders the Parliament so inferior to the growing intellect out of doors, is what has been hurting the national character and happiness, ever since we deserved the title of a nation of shop-keepers; – we mean a want of enthusiasm. We have had none of the right sort ever since the Brunswick Succession. Our litera-ture, till the French revolution excited it, was cold and common place. Our national music is so still. A painter, who should try to rouse a real feeling for his art, was and is still thought to be a kind of rebel against academies; and Sir Joshua Reynolds was frightened, and subsided in a courtier. Our war with France, as to any thing generous, was a pretence and an affectation. We had just fought America, because she struggled for real liberty; and now, out of the same fear, a junto of courtiers and money-getters fought the French. The people acquiesced, because the passion for war is always cultivated as much as possible among them by the interested, and because they were always to be roused against the French, as little boys are against one another at school – 'What! Won't you fight Jenkings?' But the truth is, they neither loved the legitimate, nor were in any pain for liberties to which they were growing unaccustomed. They had no enthu-siasm, bad or good, except for money-getting. Any turncoat made tools of them, provided he was on the jobbing side; and Pitt and

Burke made them fight and even advance money, in the hope of its being repaid with interest. But they fought to no purpose except to get jobs from Government, and drain the blood and resources of the middle gentry and the lower orders; nor would they have fought to more purpose at last, had it not been for the rashness of Bonaparte himself, whom they first encouraged to resemble their masters and then taught to despise both. The battle of Waterloo, setting aside other causes which are yet to be explained on the French side, was gained partly by passive force, and partly by some remainder of that better national spirit which our ancestors obtained for us, and which we have been losing every day. So precious are the very dregs of freedom.

This victory however contained within it some seeds of a wholesome reaction. It was obtained by popular strength, – the same weapon which has rendered the German people so sensible of their own consequence, whether against foreign or home despots. A new generation too, in the mean while was growing up; and the immediate events of the world, a new and a better school of letters, and particularly the outrageous faithlessness of the Allies to their promises, fell in as excitements to that spirit of enthusiasm, which is in some degree natural to youth. See how the youth of Germany have been venting their feelings. A similar intelligence is rapidly increasing among the younger part of the people of England. They have been taught in a less dull school than their Anti-Gallican predecessors, and in a less extreme one than the Jacobin; and are therefore neither witless nor hopeless. They need not the love of money to put an idea in their heads; nor retreat into the most selfish prejudices for comfort. Above all, they have seen what poor figures their predecessors cut as sordid traffickers, tools, and empty heads; and as is generally the case with the intelligent children of the foolish or gross, they are inclined to the very opposite tastes and opinions of their fathers.

Now the House of Commons is behind hand in this respect. Some of the leaders of it are as old or older than Mr Pitt himself would have been; and most of them, who are middle aged, were young men, spoiled by him when he was in the height of his hopes and power. The rest, generally speaking, are pretty nearly of the same age and bad habits, old hangers-on of the club-rooms, place-men and expecters of places, persons implicated with every part of a corrupt system; men with a great many wants and bad tastes, and not the spirits or strength of mind to lessen them; servants of the aristocracy and the other House; yea and nay voters with war-makers, who are ignorant of the next island in the Channel; making full Houses when the Peers and other Boroughmongers are to be maintained, more than half empty ones when the best interests of the people of England are to be brought before them, and fairly running away from the very mention of Ireland; – in short, wretched talkers when they do speak, dumb voters away of property and liberties in general, sharers of the artificial and poverty-making wealth of the paper system, and maintaining that all is well, in spite of starvation and secret imprisonment, as long as they have their horses and boots of a morning, their white waistcoat and bottle of an evening, and as few ideas in their heads as can give them trouble.

There are exceptions of course; but this description is only the sum and substance of what the persons excepted have told them over and over again to their faces, when despairing of seeing the most decent or urgent measure carried. A correspondent wonders that the men of ability and integrity in the House do not fairly get up and walk out in a body, when common sense and decency is about to be contradicted as it so often is by the votes of the majority. The idea has a good appearance; and in truth has often been before us; but there must be a much greater number of really independent men in the House, before a body of them could be either numerous or spirited enough to act in this manner, and to give it any effect. It is the people that must do the work themselves; – it is the people that must refuse to hear the daily dictatorial shallowness of the Ministers, and the hopeless and feeble opposition of a few men; – it is the people that must again render the House constitutional, intelligent, and free.

139

Let them perpetually then keep these memorandums before their thoughts: –

First, That it is hopeless to expect a Reform from *within* the House, as now constituted: –

Second, That it is their great duty as well as interest to avert if possible that alternative of which a celebrated statesman forewarned them – A Reform 'with a vengeance from without': –

Third, That the upper classes of the democracy and their traffickers are, for the most and elder part, men whose minds have been long stagnant from sordid and unenquiring habits; that they have no enthusiasm for any thing great, good, and unselfish; – none for natural and rural habits as in Elizabeth's time; none for popular liberty as in that of the Charleses; none for elegant taste and sociality as in Queen Anne's; nothing to remind them of real pleasure for themselves, or justice towards others.

Fourth and last, – That the younger as well as other more intelligent parts of the Community have felt and seen better; that circumstances have given them minds and hopes superior to those of their predecessors; that corruption and worldliness are never so corrupt, and worldly, and foolish, as when they are old; that they never atone for their sins to this world, even if they become aware of them, but only endeavour to make the best for themselves in the next; that they are too old to be taught, and too human and owing to previous circumstances to be treated vindictively; – in short, that the hopes of Reform and of all our influence upon mankind are in the hands of the younger part of the community; that you will do well to encourage them as much as you can, to get as many as possible into Parliament; and in a word, assist by every means in your power, the new growth of taste, liberality, popular feeling, and a love of nature and justice, as at once the only weapons, and the very best rewards, of your approaching victories over the dull and the sordid.

The Examiner
1 March 1818

I and We

He, I, You, And, We, It, They, affright the soul. – *Churchill*

I am very much hampered with this *I* of mine. If I value myself upon anything, it is upon being social; which is a thing essentially me. On the other hand, it is difficult to be plural, when talking of things singular: and the melody of one's prose, as I said before, is injured. *We were, We once*, and *We were once*, are vile sounds. It is the biographical gossip into which I have been led in this paper, which made me adopt the first person singular. Vivid personal recollections, especially in solitude, produce a strong sense of one's individuality. It is difficult, when we feel ourselves lonely, to fancy ourselves numerous: it is not easy, in calling to mind an exclusive thump we had at school, to imagine it distributed, as it ought to have been. Harshness, kindness, soft words that bring tears into our eyes, maternal solicitude, danger, bodily and mental pain, experiences peculiar to ourselves as members of society, or so rare as not to be common, draw portraits of us in sharp outline to our minds; and the reader will forget the injunction of Montaigne, if he thinks that the likeness is always flattering. There is an egotism of the letter, and maybe an egotism of the spirit, in writing of the first person singular. It is less equivocal to say we; and doubtless there is a greater number of modest writers who adopt that mode than the other. But a double unity nevertheless may cloak itself under the double pronoun. Scaliger, one of the most arrogant critics that ever lived, writes often in the plural number; but nobody thinks him the less arrogant for swelling and dogmatizing as he does, and laying his *Ipse dixits* about him like a couple of sticks instead of one, in the shape of a *Nos diximus*. When he tells us, speaking of the ancient dance called the Panoply, that he often danced it when a boy, at the command of his uncle Boniface, before the Emperor Maximilian, 'not without the astonishment of all Germany,' and that the Emperor used to say that 'a breast-plate must have been his skin or his cradle,' we do not the less laugh at his vanity, because he

141

speaks of himself in the plural instead of the singular number. There are men now writing in England under the guise of We, vainer than any whom a peculiarity of situation and the habit of writing the truth induce to talk of themselves occasionally in the singular. I do not pretend to be exempt from the vanity of an author; without it I should not be one. Still less do I claim exemption from the vanity of a human being: or I should not be able to be at peace with myself among so many who surpass me. But I deny by my own experience what has been so often asserted respecting everybody's content with himself, when compared with others. It is said that no man would part with his personal identity. I am sure it is not so. The difficulty would be in parting with one's old affections and friends. Make me, ye Gods, to-morrow, the healthiest young fellow in England, with competent fortune, a good heart, a liberal understanding, and contrive somehow or other to let me have my old friends, and I would take in Mr What-d'ye-call-him's Wishing-Cap with as much good natured patronage as any modest author could wish. I would give up every thing I possess, short of any good I may do with it to enable me to show two or three persons the sense I have of their kindness. But the good is problematical, though I have always enough hope of it to persevere. Were my opinion of myself greater than it is, I should be contented under any reverse of fortune with thinking of my glory, and of the effect I should have in future times upon the world. As it is, I have just enough to keep me in heart, and encourage me to take whatever good may come. As a friend of mine said, 'I have been used to myself a good number of years, and really cannot dislike myself.' But this is very different from a flattering comparison with others. Not only the troubles I have experienced, but the very gaiety of my happier hours – the very social spirits which subject a man to the charge of vanity from less acceptable tempers – have given me a sympathy with others, which enables me without pain to fancy myself identified with this or that person. After all, perhaps, this is only a dispute about words. The question is supposed to be one of personal vanity, and is nothing but a matter of habit and affection. Ye,

142

even ye, my calamities, if I could willingly forego the recollection of you, could I forego the recollection of others connected with you?

Socrates exclaimed in the market-place, 'What a number of things are here, which I do not want!' He had a right to his exclamation whether he looked on commodities or men. For my part, to say nothing of marketables, I can scarcely ever see a man above the common run, whether for intellectual or moral qualities, but I recognize in him things which I want very much. I except certain kinds of talent, because they give no comfort to the possessor. But I would give a great deal to have my poetry as fine as Mr Wordsworth's, or my prose as easy and full of matter as Elia's. The critical faculty of this friend, the imagination of another, the generous prudence of a third, and the thousand little instances of an overlooking of himself in a fourth, fill me by turns with admiration and humility. The best thing I possess is the art of giving the commonplaces of life a new gilding, and I would give up tomorrow all the praise of this for a round sum of money, if the buyer could do my work better. My demand should be less, if praise or the notion of it did not become a solid good to us fanciful authors. I should haggle more, before I parted with the faculty itself; and yet I sometimes doubt whether it has done me more good than harm; whether it has gilded more troubles for me or produced them. But this is not the question. An author is one, and his readers are many. If a greater good can be produced to the world by his troubles than without them, his lot is justified. His amount of comfort, whether for or against himself, is a comparative nothing. The world need not be frightened with stories of the calamities of authors, and of poets out at elbow. The calamities of good authors, in the first place, have not proceeded from authorship, or from want of means that way, but from qualities, bad or good, that produce calamity in all walks of life. What they have suffered, indeed, in certain high points of view, such as the calamities arising from patriotism, and other great sympathies with mankind, may be taken into account; but these are not the points upon which they are generally warned off. If a young man is bent upon being an author, let his friends see if he can earn his living by his pen. If he cannot, they are warranted in doing their best to take it from him. If he can, he is of consequence enough to society to be trusted with his own destiny. A supposed genius for poetry must be content to wait for opportunities, and should sacrifice no certainty meanwhile: especially as the greatest poetry is generally the latest understood. His spirit, if real, will make its way somehow. Let him keep his orb behind the cloud, sure that it cannot be altered by the delay, or kept there forever. If it cool, he finds himself mistaken, and no harm is done. But what are even a few mistaken men to the myriads of readers made and gladdened by authors in general? Even mistaken authorship, bad as it is, is not the only misfortune, nor the worst. The spirit which leads a man into the mistake, carries some kind of fanciful payment with it, unknown to less heroic absurdities: though to be sure, a coat out at elbows, and a bed at night in a door-way, are extremities which few people in their senses would chuse to risk.

But I am wandering from my subject. I said in the first number of the *Wishing-Cap* that it was impossible for me to sustain a fictitious character, like that of Bickerstaff and others. This was said unadvisedly: for though it is impossible for a man to keep himself unknown, if he has been known at all (as Steele found it) he may take a fictitious signature, and so be as egotistical as he pleases without the charge of it. But I have a sense of truth that haunts me in the most literal shape; perhaps because my love of fiction (which is quite as strong in its way) is not to be trusted out of the pale of a scrupulous veracity. I remember when I first went to school, some of the boys told such prodigious histories of their lives and adventures that I was tempted to try my arm in that bow of Ulysses; and I believe I have ever since been frightened by my success. My nicety is the greater, inasmuch as from conflicting pursuits, a salient imagination, and occasional prostrations of health, I have been a considerable promise-breaker in my time, though with every intention of keeping my word at the moment I gave it. I had once occasion to observe that this trenched upon my reputation for veracity with a person for whom I have a great affection; which gave me such a pang that should anyone call in question the least thing I utter, he will become liable to as great an indignation and bitterness as if I were in the wrong. I do not believe I was ever guilty of a fault for which I have not severely suffered; but to give a hint to our humanities in this world, deeper than what I shall here stop to discuss, the nature of things makes us suffer now and then for our virtues as well as our faults; and not the least of my troubles has been owing to the love of truth. They are almost the only ones with which I could not have heartily dispensed. But to suffer for our virtues enables us to endure and amend the other part of us.

Another reason for my adopting the use of the singular person, is the interest I take in anecdotes related of themselves by other writers. *I* seems more natural to these in proportion as *We* would be unnatural in a private society. A man does not say at table, 'We once got a bruise on our knee'; or, 'When we walk out, we always put our book in our pocket,' I have been accustomed to chat with the readers of the *Examiner* so long and so familiarly that I feel present, as of old, at their breakfasts and firesides. A fictitious name warrants a fictitious character; but though the humours of the latter, false or true, are often entertaining, and many contain an essence of truth applicable to humanity at large, superior to anything related by matter of fact people, yet it is not only impossible to take an equal interest in it, but matter of fact, if not absolutely ill told, will render almost anybody's writing interesting. We can never be sure of the others: but a man who speaks in his own name makes a demand on our behalf, and must deserve it or abide by the consequence.

Nevertheless, when an author who speaks in the first person singular is well known, and has engaged himself to write nothing but what is true, he may certainly use the singular or plural number as he pleases; and I shall accordingly take the liberty (somewhat strange, I confess) of saying *I* or *We* according as the impulse comes upon me. If I am telling a story as at table among friends, I shall most likely be tempted to speak as I am accustomed. If I think collectively as a part of their society, or am engaged in speculating upon some general point of reflection, or in short have something to say which does not require a certain biographical zest in the telling, then I shall most likely be *We*. I do not bind myself. Perhaps I may or may not, when I come to the point. All that I wish is to have the choice of doing so, and to be thought meanwhile not more deficient in modesty than I am. When I was a youth, and grew vain of having readers, I said *I* out of ostentation. Afterwards, becoming a little wiser, I said *We*; and now, whether I am wiser or not, it is indifferent to me whether I say *I* or *We*, provided the reader is equally disposed to hear me, and he and I can do each other any good....

The Examiner
13 June 1824

A 'Now'
DESCRIPTIVE OF A HOT DAY

'The paper that was most liked by Keats, if I remember, was the one on a hot summer's day, entitled *A Now*. He was with me when I was writing and reading it to him, and contributed one or two of the passages.' – *Autobiography*, Chapter 16

Now the rosy – (and lazy –) fingered Aurora, issuing from her saffron house, calls up the moist vapours to surround her, and goes veiled with them as long as she can; till Phœbus, coming forth in his power, looks everything out of the sky, and holds sharp, uninterrupted empire from his throne of beams. Now the mower begins to make his sweeping cuts more slowly, and resorts often to the beer. Now the carter sleeps a-top of his load of hay, or plods with double slouch of shoulder, looking out with eyes winking under his shading hat, and with a hitch upward of one side of his mouth. Now the little girl at her grandmother's cottage-

146

door watches the coaches go by, with her hand held up over her sunny forehead. Now labourers look well, resting in their white shirts at the doors of rural ale-houses. Now an elm is fine there, with a seat under it; and horses drink out of the trough, stretching their yearning necks with loosened collars; and the traveller calls for his glass of ale, having been without one for more than ten minutes; and his horse stands wincing at the flies, giving sharp shivers of his skin, and moving to and fro his ineffectual docked tail; and now Miss Betty Wilson, the host's daughter, comes streaming forth in a flowered gown and ear-rings, carrying with four of her beautiful fingers the foaming glass, for which, after the traveller has drank it, she receives with an indifferent eye, looking another way, the lawful twopence. Now grasshoppers 'fry,' as Dryden says.[1] Now cattle stand in water, and ducks are envied. Now boots, and shoes, and trees by the road-side, are thick with dust; and dogs, rolling in it, after issuing out of the water, into which they have been thrown to fetch sticks, come scattering horror among the legs of the spectators. Now a fellow who finds he has three miles further to go in a pair of tight shoes is in a pretty situation. Now rooms with the sun upon them become intolerable; and the apothecary's apprentice, with a bitterness beyond aloes, thinks of the pond he used to bathe in at school. Now men with powdered heads (especially if thick) envy those that are unpowdered, and stop to wipe them up hill, with countenances that seem to expostulate with destiny. Now boys assemble round the village pump with a ladle to it, and delight to make a forbidden splash and get wet through the shoes. Now also they make suckers of leather, and bathe all day long in rivers and ponds, and make mighty fishings for 'tittle-bats'. Now the bee, as he hums along, seems to be talking heavily of the heat. Now doors and brick-walls are burning to the hand; and a walled lane, with dust and broken bottles in it, near a brick-field, is a thing not to be thought of. Now a green lane, on the contrary, thick-set with hedge-row elms, and having the noise of a brook 'rumbling in pebble-stone', is one of the pleasantest things in the world.

147

Now, in town, gossips talk more than ever to one another, in rooms, in door-ways, and out of window, always beginning the conversation with saying that the heat is overpowering. Now blinds are let down, and doors thrown open, and flannel waist-coats left off, and cold meat preferred to hot, and wonder expressed why tea continues so refreshing, and people delight to sliver lettuces into bowls, and apprentices water door-ways with tin canisters that lay several atoms of dust. Now the water-cart, jumbling along the middle of the street, and jolting the showers out of its box of water, really does something. Now fruiterers' shops and dairies look pleasant, and ices are the only things to those who can get them. Now ladies loiter in baths; and people make presents of flowers; and wine is put into ice; and the after-dinner lounger recreates his head with applications of perfumed water out of long-necked bottles. Now the lounger, who cannot resist riding his new horse, feels his boots burn him. Now buck-skins are not the lawn of Cos.[2] Now jockeys, walking in great-coats to lose flesh, curse inwardly. Now five fat people in a stage-coach hate the sixth fat one who is coming in, and think he has no right to be so large. Now clerks in offices do nothing but drink soda-water and spruce-beer, and read the newspaper. Now the old-clothesman drops his solitary cry more deeply into the areas on the hot and forsaken side of the street; and bakers look vicious; and cooks are aggravated; and the steam of a tavern-kitchen catches hold of us like the breath of Tartarus. Now delicate skins are beset with gnats; and boys make their sleeping companion start up, with playing a burning-glass on his hand; and black-smiths are super-carbonated; and cobblers in their stalls almost feel a wish to be transplanted; and butter is too easy to spread; and the dragoons wonder whether the Romans liked their hel-mets; and old ladies, with their lappets unpinned, walk along in a state of dilapidation; and the servant maids are afraid they look vulgarly hot; and the author, who has a plate of strawberries brought him, finds that he has come to the end of his writing.

The Indicator
1820

148

A 'Now'

'Now, all amid the rigours of the year.' – Thomson

A friend tells us, that having written a 'Now,' descriptive of a hot day, we ought to write another, descriptive of a cold one; and accordingly we do so. It happens that we are, at this minute, in a state at once fit and unfit for the task, being in the condition of the little boy at school, who, when asked the Latin for 'cold,' said he had it 'at his finger's ends;' but this helps us to set off with a right taste of our subject; and the fire, which is clicking in our ear, shall soon enable us to handle it comfortably in other respects.

Now, then, to commence. – But first, the reader who is good-natured enough to have a regard for these papers, may choose to be told of the origin of the use of this word Now, in case he is not already acquainted with it. It was suggested to us by the striking convenience it affords to descriptive writers, such as Thomson and others, who are fond of beginning their paragraphs with it, thereby saving themselves a world of trouble in bringing about a nicer conjunction of the various parts of their subject.

Now when the first foul torrent of the brooks –
Now flaming up to heaven the potent sun –
Now when the cheerless empire of the sky –
But now –
When now –
Where now –
For now – etc.

We say nothing of similar words among other nations, or of a certain *But* of the Greeks which was as useful to them on all occasions as the *And so* of the little children's stories. Our business is with our old indigenous friend. No other *Now* can be so present, so instantaneous, so extremely *Now*, as our own Now. The now of the Latins – *Nunc*, or *Jam*, as he sometimes calls himself – is a fellow of past ages. He is no Now. And the *Nun* of the Greek is

149

older. How can there be a *Now* which was *Then*? a *'Now-then,'* as we sometimes barbarously phrase it. 'Now *and* then' is intelligible; but 'Now-then' is an extravagance, fit only for the delicious moments of a gentleman about to crack his bottle, or to run away with a lady, or to open a dance, or to carve a turkey, and chine, or to pelt snow-balls, or to commit some other piece of ultra-vivacity, such as excuses a man from the nicer proprieties of language.

But to begin.

Now the moment people wake in the morning they perceive the coldness with their faces, though they are warm with their bodies, and exclaim 'Here's a day!' and pity the poor little sweep, and the boy with the water-cresses. How anybody can go to a cold ditch, and gather water-cresses, seems marvellous. Perhaps we hear great lumps in the street of something falling; and, looking through the window, perceive the roofs of the neighbouring houses thick with snow. The breath is visible, issuing from the mouth as we lie. Now we hate getting up, and hate shaving, and hate the empty grate in one's bed-room; and water freezes in ewers, and you may set the towel upright on its own hardness, and the window-panes are frost-whitened, or it is foggy, and the sun sends a dull, brazen beam into one's room; or, if it is fine, the windows outside are stuck with icicles; or a detestable thaw has begun, and they drip; but, at all events, it is horribly cold, and delicate shavers fidget about their chambers, looking distressed, and cherish their hard-hearted enemy, the razor, in their bosoms, to warm him a little, and coax him into a consideration of their chins. Savage is a cut, and makes them think destiny really too hard.

Now breakfast is fine; and the fire seems to laugh at us as we enter the breakfast-room, and say, 'Ha! ha! here's a better room than the bed-chamber!' and we always poke it before we do anything else; and people grow selfish about seats near it; and little boys think their elders tyrannical for saying, 'Oh, *you* don't want the fire; your blood is young.' And truly that is not the way of stating the case, albeit young blood is warmer than old. Now the butter is too hard to spread; and the rolls and toast are at their maximum; and the former look glorious as they issue smoking out of the flannel in which they come from the baker's; and people who come with single knocks at the door are pitied; and the voices of boys are loud in the street, sliding or throwing snow-balls; and the dustman's bell sounds cold; and we wonder how anybody can go about selling fish, especially with that hoarse voice; and school-boys hate their slates, and blow their fingers, and detest infinitely the no-fire at school; and the parish-beadle's nose is redder than ever.

Now sounds in general are dull, and smoke out of chimneys looks warm and rich, and birds are pitied, hopping about for crumbs, and the trees look wiry and cheerless, albeit they are still beautiful to imaginative eyes, especially the evergreens, and the birch with boughs like dishevelled hair. Now mud in roads is stiff, and the kennel ices over, and boys make illegal slides in the pathways, and ashes are strewed before doors; or you crunch the snow as you tread, or kick mud-flakes before you, or are horribly muddy in cities. But if it is a hard frost, all the world is buttoned up and great-coated, except ostentatious elderly gent-lemen, and pretended beggars with naked feet; and the delicious sound of 'All hot' is heard from roasted apple and potato stalls, the vendor himself being cold, in spite of his 'hot,' and stamping up and down to warm his feet; and the little boys are astonished to think how he can eat bread and cold meat for his dinner, instead of the smoking apples.

Now skaters are on the alert; the cutlers' shop-windows abound with their swift shoes; and as you approach the scene of action (pond or canal) you hear the dull grinding noise of the skates to and fro, and see tumbles, and Banbury cake-men and blackguard boys playing 'hockey,' and ladies standing shivering on the banks, admiring anybody but their brother, especially the gentleman who is cutting figures of eight, who, for his part, is admiring his own figure. Beginners affect to laugh at their tum-bles, but are terribly angry, and long to thump the by-standers. On thawing days, idlers persist to the last in skating or sliding amidst the slush and bending ice, making the Humane-Society man ferocious. He feels as if he could give them the deaths from which it is his business to save them. When you have done skating you come away, feeling at once warm and numb in the feet, from the tight effect of the skates; and you carry them with an ostentatious air of indifference, as if you had done wonders; whereas you have fairly had three slips, and can barely achieve the inside edge.

Now riders look sharp, and horses seem brittle in the legs, and old gentlemen feel so; and coachmen, cabmen, and others, stand swinging their arms across at their sides to warm themselves; and blacksmiths' shops look pleasant, and potato shops detestable; the fishmongers' still more so. We wonder how he can live in that plash of wet and cold fish without even a window. Now clerks in offices envy the one next the fire-place; and men from behind counters hardly think themselves repaid by being called out to speak to a countess in her chariot; and the wheezy and effeminate pastry-cook, hatless and aproned, and with his hand in his breeches-pocket (as the graphic Cruikshank noticeth in his almanack)[1] stands outside his door, chilling his household warmth with attending to the ice which is brought him, and seeing it unloaded into his cellar like coals. Comfortable look the Miss Joneses, coming this way with their muffs and furs; and the baker pities the maid-servant cleaning the steps, who, for her part, says she is not cold, which he finds it difficult to believe.

Now dinner rejoiceth the gatherers together, and cold meat is despised, and the gout defieth the morrow, thinking it but reasonable on such a day to inflame itself with 't'other bottle;' and the sofa is wheeled round to the fire after dinner, and people proceed to burn their legs in their boots, and little boys their faces; and young ladies are tormented between the cold and their complexions, and their fingers freeze at the pianoforte, but they must not say so, because it will vex their poor, comfortable grand-aunt, who is sitting with her knees in the fire, and who is so anxious that they should not be spoilt.

Now the muffin-bell soundeth sweetly in the streets, reminding us, not of the man, but his muffins, and of twilight, and evening, and curtains, and the fireside. Now play-goers get cold feet, and invalids stop up every crevice in their rooms, and make themselves worse; and the streets are comparatively silent; and the wind rises and falls in moanings; and the fire burns blue and crackles; and an easy-chair with your feet by it on a stool, the lamp or candles a little behind you, and an interesting book just opened where you left off, is a bit of heaven upon earth. People in cottages crowd close into the chimney, and tell stories of ghosts and murders, the blue flame affording something like evidence of the facts.

'The owl, with all her feathers, is a-cold,' or you think her so. The whole country feels like a petrifaction of slate and stillness, cut across by the wind; and nobody in the mail-coach is warm but the horses, who steam pitifully when they stop. The 'oldest man' makes a point of never having 'seen such weather.' People have a painful doubt whether they have any chins or not; ears ache with the wind; and the waggoner, setting his teeth together, goes puckering up his cheeks, and thinking the time will never arrive when he shall get to the Five Bells.

At night, people become sleepy with the fireside, and long to go to bed, yet fear it on account of the different temperature of the bed-room; which is furthermore apt to wake them up. Warming pans and hot-water bottles are in request; and naughty boys eschew their night-shirts, and go to bed in their socks.

'Yes,' quoth a little boy, to whom we read this passage, 'and make their younger brother go to bed first.'

The Indicator
1820

To Marianne Kent[1]

Gainsborough, Thursday, Feb. 1806

Dearest Girl, – My journey to Doncaster is deferred till next week, so I sit down to write to you a day earlier than I intended, in order that you may have two letters instead of one this week, to make up for former deficiencies. A very heavy rain last night has made the snow vanish from the fields, which looked delightfully green this morning: I walked out to enjoy the lively air and the universal sunshine, and seated myself with a book on a gateway at the bottom of a little eminence covered with evergreens, a little way from Gainsborough. It seemed the return of spring: a flock of sheep were grazing before me, and cast up every now and then their inquiring visages, as much as to say, 'What singular being is that so intent upon the mysterious thin substances he is turning over with his paws!' – The crows at intervals came wheeling with long cawings above my head, the herds lowed from the surrounding farms, the windmills whirled to the breeze, flinging their huge and rapid shadows over the fields, and the river Trent sparkled in the sun from east to west. A delightful serenity diffused itself through my heart: I worshipped the magnificence and the love of the God of Nature, and I thought of you;: these two sensations always arise in my heart in the quiet of a rural landscape, and I have often considered it a proof of the purity and the reality of my affection for you, that it always feels most powerful in my religious moments. And it is very natural. Are you not the greatest blessing Heaven has bestowed upon me? Your image attends me not only in my rural rambles, not only in those healthful walks when, escaped from the clamour of streets and the glare of theatres, I am ready to exclaim with Cowper,

'God made the country, and man made the town.'

It is present with me even in the bustle of life: it gives me a distaste to frivolous and riotous society; it excites me to improve myself in order to preserve your affection, and it quenches the

154

little flashes of caprice and impatience which disturb the repose of existence. If I feel my anger rising at trifles, it checks me instantaneously: it seems to say to me, 'Why do you disturb yourself? Marian loves you: you deserve her love, and you ought to be above these little marks of a little mind.' Such is the power of a virtuous love. I am naturally a man of violent passions, but your affection has taught me to subdue them. Whenever you feel any little disquietudes or impatience rising in your bosom, think of the happiness you bestow upon me, and real love will produce the same effects in you as it has produced in me. No reasoning person ought to marry who cannot say, 'My love has made me better and more desirous of improvement than I have been!'

I am glad to hear nothing more has been said of my standing godfather to Mr Robertson's child. I should undoubtedly excuse myself, and not only to him, but to any other acquaintance. To stand godfather is, I know, reckoned a very trifling ceremony: people ask it of others, either to gratify their own vanity or that of the person asked; they think nothing of the Heaven whom they are about to invoke. It is looked upon as a mere gossiping entertainment: a few child's squalls, a few mumbled amens, and a few mumbled cakes, and a few smirks accompanied by a few fees, and it is all over. The character and the peculiar faith of the promisers have nothing to do with it: the child's interest has nothing to do with it; the person most benefited is the parson, who is thinking all the time what sort of a present he shall get. Now, observe what I must do, should I undertake to be a godfather. I must come into the presence of God, a presence not to be slighted though in a private room, to worship him with a falsehood in my mouth, that is, to make him a profession of faith which I do not understand; I must then promise him to teach the child the very faith which I do not understand, and to guard her youth from evil ways; when it is very probable I shall never be with her or see her, and most likely, if I did see her, I should get my head broken by her relations for giving impertinent advice. Considered in itself, I think the idea of christening a child and answering for what one cannot possibly foresee, a very ridiculous

155

one; but when Heaven is called upon and the presence of the Deity invoked to witness it, it becomes a serious ceremony though it may be an erroneous one, and the invocation of the Deity is not to be sported with even on an erroneous occasion. I should go with respect into the society of any sect at worship – Mahometans, Christians, or Jews: I should feel a veneration for the cause of their worship, though not for the manner. My brother Stephen, an orthodox man, selected, as godfather and godmother for his son, a free-living and free-thinking old colonel who never spoke well of the church, and the colonel's daughter, his present wife, who never went there; but then, you know, the child's godfather was a colonel, and his godmother a colonel's daughter! My brother John, a Deist, was content to make his children virtuous; and leaving them to settle what it is impossible for him to settle for them, never christened them at all. I am afraid I tire your patience, my dear girl, upon this orthodox subject; but I say this much to you under the hope that you yourself will be cautious how you enter into engagements of this sort. Let us do as much as possible for children at all times, and teach them the little we can; but let us not call Heaven to witness what we neither may be able nor willing to do for them. . . . .

To Marianne Hunt

Trinity College, Cambridge
Sunday, 6 January 1811

. . . Cambridge improves upon me at every turn; and I meet, everywhere, with respect and hospitality. To-day I dine with Wood, an old schoolfellow and patron of mine, who is tutor at Pembroke Hall and a Fellow also, that is to say, he enjoys rooms and a regular stipend from the college, and does what he pleases. These Fellows are absolute monks, without monkish superstition or restraint; they live luxuriously, walk, ride, read, and have nothing to get, in this world, but a good appetite of a morning. Yesterday I was in the chapel of this magnificent college, Trinity; at one end of it there is a statue of Newton by Roubilliac, full of thought and dignity; and at the other, over the altar, a painting of St Michael trampling on Satan, by West. You may conceive the pleasure this latter circumstance gave me; it seemed, in some measure, to make me belong to the place: not that I regret altogether the not having been at college, for otherwise I should not have been so soon out in the world; and after all, London, as Goldsmith says, is the first of universities. It must be confessed, however, though you will not discover it in this dull letter, that Trinity College is full of inspiration, having educated Newton, Bacon, Dryden, Cowley, &c; possessing libraries and other buildings like palaces, and having at the back one of the most rural walks and prospects in the county, – the river Cam running through shelving banks of grass, upon which, in the summertime, you may literally lie down, to the water's edge, with your book and your pencil.

Trinity College, 8 January 1811

The weather at Cambridge is still piercingly cold, but the wind has abated, and we have fine sunshine days and moon-light evenings. Were the weather a little less severe, I can conceive nothing finer than walking round the cloisters of the smaller court of this college on such evenings. Even our cloisters at school, when the gates were shut in, had a very inspiring effect at such a time; they were twice as long as those of Westminster School, but the cloisters here are still longer, besides being twice as broad as Christ's, with a prospect on one side of trees and the river Cam, and the recollection of all the great men who have trodden them in the bloom of youth and genius. The other night I went to the chapel and heard the service, which is not only imposing, but something more, if you can get rid of the idea that the persons

157

about you regard it as a mere task. The men attend in surplices; there is an excellent organ and set of choristers; wax-lights and boughs of the box-tree are fixed alternately down the long reading-desks; and the chanting and anthems perfectly bear one away from earth. As for me, I was in the dean's seat, with my head just peering above a gorgeous cushion and huge psalm-book; and wanted nothing but a cowl and crucifix to be a complete monk on the occasion: not that I felt inclined to give up the world and its delight, any more than the monks themselves – beauty of every kind, *poeticized*, comes into the composition of my heaven – beauty of thinking, beauty of feeling, beauty of talking, beauty of hearing, and, of course, beauty of seeing, including visions of beautiful eyes and beautiful turns of limb. But this you knew long ago. This morning I visited Trinity Library, as I did yesterday that of Pembroke Hall and of the University. It is, like all the other buildings of this college, complete inside and out, and of a classical magnificence. The floor is of marble; the room 200 feet long and 40 broad; the bookcases, which are ranged at the sides, in the manner of stables, are of oak, and the projections are each surmounted with a bust of some great literary man. Several of these busts are by Roubilliac. 'This,' says I to Scholefield, 'is the place for Mrs Hunt to see.' 'Ay, sir, then she would be altogether happy, no doubt.' Among some of the curiosities here, are a pair of Queen Elizabeth's shoes, which, if they fitted her, must have belonged to formidable feet. They are placed by the side of a Chinese pair, which are just as long as their quarterings, and of proportionate narrowness. They look like an infant's; but luckily there is a model of the feet to which they belong, and never was anything so hideous! The four lesser toes are bent under the sole, just as you would bend four fingers of your hand into the palm, so that nothing but the great toe is left; and the foot altogether looks exactly like a hoof of flesh terminated by a claw. I would fain have relieved myself by the sight of a truly noble curiosity in another part of the room – the original of Milton's own hand-writing; but it was maliciously locked up. So much for *our* chapel and library, for I am already a Trinity man in my likings as well as

158

my lodgings. I forgot to tell you, however, that I have at last procured what I have so long wished for in vain – a book of chants to copy. I prosecute the task devoutly, and mean to lift up my voice, when I return, like any Luther. By-the-by, you never told me how the books and music arrived. Pray do not forget to put the latter in tune, and take care of my Handel. I enclose two letters, which Mrs Hunter will have the goodness to give Mr Button for me. Fireside remembrances. You will see me again certainly on Saturday night. I hope my little boy will not have forgotten me. Your affectionate   Henry

To Mr Ives

Surrey Jail, 5 February 1813

Mr Leigh Hunt presents his compliments to Mr Ives, and puts down his wishes upon paper as requested.

His first and greatest wish, then, is to be allowed to have his wife and children living with him in the prison. It is to be observed, that his is a new case within these walls; and not only so, but that his habits have always been of the most domestic kind, that he has not been accustomed to be from home a day long, and that he is subject, particularly at night-time, to violent attacks of illness, accompanied with palpitations of the heart and other nervous affections, which render a companion not only much wanted, but sometimes hardly to be dispensed with. His state of health is bad at the present moment, as everybody may see; not so bad indeed as it has been, and he wishes to make no parade of it; but quite bad enough to make him feel tenfold all the wants of his situation, and to render it absolutely necessary that his greatest comforts should not all be taken away. If he would take time, however, to consider this request, his next wish is that his wife and children be allowed to be with him in the daytime. His happiness is wound up in them, and he shall say no more on this subject except that a total separation in respect of abode would be almost as bad to him as tearing his body asunder.

His third and last request is, that his friends be allowed to come up to his room during the daytime; and if this permission be given, he will give his word that it shall not be abused. His physician has often declared that society is necessary to his health; but though he has been used to every comfort that domestic and social happiness can bestow, he is content with as little as possible, and provided his just wish be granted, could make almost any sacrifice.

This is all he has to say on the subject, and all with which he should every trouble anybody. The hope of living in Mr Ives's house he has given up; many privations, of course, he is prepared to endure; with the other regulations of the prison he has no wish to interfere; and from what little has already been seen of him in this place, he believes that every credit will be given him for conducting himself in a reasonable and gentlemanly manner; for as he is a stubborn enemy of what is wrong, so is he one of the quietest and most considerate of friends of what is right. He has many private friends who would do their utmost for him; and his character, he believes, has procured him some public ones of the highest description, who would leave no means untaken for bettering his condition, but he would willingly leave his comforts to those about him. To conclude, he is prepared to suffer all extremities rather than do himself dishonour; but it is no dishonour to have the feelings of a husband and a father; and till he is dead to them and to everything else, he shall not cease exerting himself on their behalf.

From the *Autobiography*

The tipstaves prepared me for a singular character in my gaoler. His name was Ives. I was told he was a very self-willed personage, not the more accommodating for being in a bad state of health; and that he called everybody *Mister*. 'In short,' said one of the tipstaves, 'he is one as may be led, but he'll never be *druv.'*

The sight of the prison gate and the high wall was a dreary business.[1] I thought of my horseback and the downs of Brighton; but congratulated myself, at all events, that I had come thither with a good conscience. After waiting in the prison yard as long as if it had been the anteroom of a minister, I was ushered into the presence of the great man. He was in his parlour, which was decently furnished, and he had a basin of broth before him, which he quitted on my appearance, and rose with much solemnity to meet me. He seemed about fifty years of age. He had a white night-cap on, as if he was going to be hanged, and a great red face, which looked as if he had been hanged already, or were ready to burst with blood. Indeed, he was not allowed by his physician to speak in a tone above a whisper.

The first thing which this dignified person said was, 'Mister, I'd ha' given a matter of a hundred pounds, that you had not come to this place – a hundred pounds!' The emphasis which he had laid on the word 'hundred' was ominous.

I forget what I answered. I endeavoured to make the best of the matter; but he recurred over and over again to the hundred pounds; and said he wondered, for his part, what the Government meant by sending me there, for the prison was not a prison fit for a gentleman. He often repeated this opinion afterwards, adding, with a peculiar nod of his head, 'And, Mister, they knows it.'

I said, that if a gentleman deserved to be sent to prison, he ought not to be treated with a greater nicety than anyone else: upon which he corrected me, observing very properly (though, as the phrase is, it was one word for the gentleman and two for the letter of prison lodgings), that a person who had been used to a better mode of living than 'low people' was not treated with the same justice, if forced to lodge exactly as they did.

I told him his observation was very true; which gave him a favourable opinion of my understanding; for I had many occasions of remarking, that he looked upon nobody as his superior, speaking even of members of the royal family as persons whom he knew very well, and whom he estimated at no higher rate than became him. One royal duke had lunched in his parlour, and another he had laid under some polite obligation. 'They knows me', said he, 'very well, Mister; and, Mister, I knows them.' This concluding sentence he uttered with great particularity and precision.

He was not proof, however, against a Greek Pindar, which he happened to light upon one day among my books. Its unintelligible character gave him a notion that he had got somebody to deal with, who might really know something which he did not. Perhaps the gilt leaves and red morocco binding had their share in the magic. The upshot was, that he always showed himself anxious to appear well with me, as a clever fellow, treating me with great civility on all occasions but one, when I made him very angry by disappointing him in a money amount. The Pindar was a mystery that staggered him. I remember very well, that giving me a long account one day of something connected with his business, he happened to catch with his eye the shelf that contained it, and, whether he saw it or not, abruptly finished by observing, 'But, Mister, you knows all these things as well as I do.'...

I now applied to the magistrates for permission to have my wife and children constantly with me, which was granted. Not so my request to move into the gaoler's house. Mr Holme Sumner, on occasion of a petition from a subsequent prisoner, told the House of Commons that my room had a view over the Surrey hills, and that I was very well content with it. I could not feel obliged to him for this postliminous piece of enjoyment, especially when I remembered that he had done all in his power to prevent my removal out of the room, precisely (as it appeared to us) because it looked upon nothing but the felons, and because I was *not* contented. In fact, you could not see out of the windows at all, without getting on a chair; and then, all that you saw was the miserable men whose chains had been clanking from daylight. The perpetual sound of these chains wore upon my spirits in a manner to which my state of health allowed me reasonably to object. The yard, also, in which I took exercise, was very small.

162

The gaoler proposed that I should be allowed to occupy apartments in his house, and walk occasionally in the prison garden; adding, that I should certainly die if I did not; and his opinion was seconded by that of the medical man. Mine host was sincere in this, if in nothing else. Telling us, one day, how warmly he had put it to the magistrates, and how he insisted that I should not survive, he turned round upon me, and, to the doctor's astonishment, added, 'Nor, Mister, will you.' I believe it was the opinion of many; but Mr Holme Sumner argued otherwise; perhaps, from his own sensations, which were sufficiently iron. Perhaps he concluded, also, like a proper old Tory, that if I did not think fit to flatter the magistrates a little, and play the courtier, my wants could not be very great. At all events, he came up one day with the rest of them, and after bowing to my wife, and piteously pinching the cheek of an infant in her arms, went down and did all he could to prevent our being comfortably situated.

The doctor then proposed that I should be removed into the prison infirmary; and this proposal was granted. Infirmary had, I confess, an awkward sound, even to my ears. I fancied a room shared with other sick persons, not the best fitted for companions; but the good-natured doctor (his name was Dixon) undeceived me. The infirmary was divided into four wards, with as many small rooms attached to them. The two upper wards were occupied, but the two on the floor had never been used: and one of these, not very providently (for I had not yet learned to think of money), I turned into a noble room. I papered the walls with a trellis of roses; I had the ceiling coloured with clouds and sky; the barred windows I screened with Venetian blinds; and when my bookcases were set up with their busts, and flowers and a pianoforte made their appearance, perhaps there was not a handsomer room on that side of the water. I took a pleasure, when a stranger knocked at the door, to see him come in and stare about him. The surprise on issuing from the Borough, and passing through the avenues of a gaol, was dramatic. Charles Lamb declared there was no other such room, except in a fairy tale.

But I possessed another surprise; which was a garden. There

163

was a little yard outside the room, railed off from another belonging to the neighbouring ward. This yard I shut in with green palings, adorned it with a trellis, bordered it with a thick bed of earth from a nursery, and even contrived to have a grass-plot. The earth I filled with flowers and young trees. There was an apple tree, from which we managed to get a pudding the second year. As to my flowers, they were allowed to be perfect. Thomas Moore, who came to see me with Lord Byron, told me had seen no such heart's-ease. . . .

My friends were allowed to be with me till ten o'clock at night, when the under-turnkey, a young man with his lantern, and much ambitious gentility of deportment, came to see them out. I believe we scattered an urbanity about the prison, till then unknown. Even William Hazlitt, who there first did me the honour of a visit, would stand interchanging amenities at the threshold, which I had great difficulty in making him pass. I know not which kept his hat off with the greater pertinacity of deference, I to the diffident cutter-up of Tory dukes and kings, or he to the amazing prisoner and invalid who issued out of a bower of roses. There came my old friends and schoolfellows, Pitman, whose wit and animal spirits have still kept him alive; Mitchell, now no more, who translated Aristophanes; and Barnes, gone too, who always reminded me of Fielding. It was he that introduced me to the late Mr Thomas Alsager,[2] the kindest of neighbours, a man of business, who contrived to be a scholar and a musician. Alsager loved his leisure, and yet would start up at a moment's notice to do the least of a prisoner's biddings!

My now old friend, Cowden Clarke,[3] with his ever young and wise heart, was good enough to be his own introducer, paving his way, like a proper visitor of prisons, with baskets of fruit.

The Lambs came to comfort me in all weathers, hail or sunshine, in daylight and in darkness, even in the dreadful frost and snow of the beginning of 1814. . . .

To evils I have owed some of my greatest blessings. It was imprisonment that brought me acquainted with my friend of friends, Shelley. I had seen little of him before; but he wrote to

164

me, making me a princely offer, which at that time I stood in no need of.[4]

Some other persons, not at all known to us, offered to raise money enough to pay the fine of £1,000. We declined it, with proper thanks; and it became us to do so. But, as far as my own feelings were concerned, I have no merit; for I was destitute, at that time, of even a proper instinct with regard to money. It was not long afterwards that I was forced to call upon friendship for its assistance; and nobly (as I shall show by and by) was it afforded me. . . .

It was very slowly that I recovered anything like a sensation of health. The bitterest evil I suffered was in consequence of having been confined so long in one spot. The habit stuck to me on my return home in a very extraordinary manner; and, I fear, some of my friends thought me ungrateful. They did me an injustice; but it was not their fault, nor could I wish them the bitter experience which alone makes us acquainted with the existence of strange things. This weakness I outlived; but I have never thoroughly recovered the shock given my constitution. My natural spirits, however, have always struggled hard to see me reasonably treated. Many things give me exquisite pleasure which seem to affect other men in a very minor degree; and I enjoyed, after all, such happy moments with my friends, even in prison, that in the midst of the beautiful climate which I afterwards visited, I was sometimes in doubt whether I would not rather have been in gaol than in Italy.

To John Keats

Mortimer Terrace
[August 1820]

Giovanni mio,   I shall see you this afternoon, & most probably every day. You judge rightly when you think I shall be glad at your putting up awhile where you are, instead of that solitary place.[1] There are humanities in the house; & if wisdom loves to live with children round her knees (the tax-gatherer apart), sick wisdom, I think, should love to live with arms about its waist. I need not say how you gratify me by the impulse which led you to write a particular sentence in your letter,[2] for you must have seen by this time how much I am attached to yourself.

I am indicating at as dull a rate as a bettered finger-post in wet weather. Not that I am ill: for I am very well altogether.   Your affectionate friend,   Leigh Hunt

To Percy Bysshe Shelley

Vale of Health, Hampstead
1 March 1821

My dearest Friend, – When you hear that this week has been the first in which I have written any politics in the *Examiner*, or anything but paragraphs in the *Indicator*, for three or four months, you will hold me more excused than I am to myself for not writing sooner to Italy. I have indeed had a hard bout of it this time; and if the portrait you have with you sympathised with my appearance, like those magic glasses in romance, the patience you found in it ought at least to look twice as great, and the checks twice as small. You know how the pressure which was left upon me, and my wish not to trouble my friends again, or rather to do them justice and myself the proper good, induced me to double my writing and set up the *Indicator*. Unluckily my anxiety had not strengthened me for the task; my animal spirits, however, revived, especially with the success of the work; but *again* I did a very foolish thing – I neglected my exercise, and was obliged occasionally to recruit myself with wine. I could not treat myself thus artificially, while I was drawing so constantly upon my faculties, for nothing. Exhaustion tempted me into excitement; excitement and work threw me back again into exhaustion; and at last

I seemed as if I were going to break up at once, body and mind. Luckily, I retained a saving knowledge as to the mode of cure. With the necessity of leaving off feverish stimulants, came a greater necessity of putting myself in motion. The more I exercised, the more I removed the natural indolence of my former state of health; and though I have gone through pangs infernal in the process, and been obliged, whenever I was not on my feet, to sit, with as stony a patience as I could get into, and let melancholy crumble away my cheeks, yet the persevering all the while in as natural a mode of living as possible, not only helped me to keep a glimpse of hope in my eyes, but has at last I think, put me into a more *promising* state of health than I have enjoyed a long while. I am sufficiently nervous still; I should be so even with the recollection of the ideas that have gone through my head; but they are diminishing daily; I again begin to enjoy intervals of forgetfulness to everything but my books and the trees; what hurt my health did no injury to my finances, and though they suffered by my leaving off writing so long, you need have no anxiety on that score. You will be sorry to hear that my brother has been found 'guilty' of standing by the constitution, by a ministerial jury; but you will be refreshed at hearing that I had for some time withdrawn from the proprietorship of the paper by his particular wish, in order that the Government might not be able to imprison both of us at once. I consented at last with the less scruple, not only because my health was the more precarious, but because my brother's name is obliged to be at the bottom of the paper as printer, and printers, though not editors, are indictable, like proprietors. Unfortunately, my brother himself has had a severe illness, but he got better in time to make an admirable defence, which you will see in the *Examiner*, together with the strong effect it had on the jury. We have two grounds also for hoping a new trial, and at all events do not expect that his imprisonment will be long, as the Government, however savage, are willing to get what popularity they can just now, and there is a coronation coming. You must excuse a letter all about myself, after the one I have just received from you; and not only so, but Marina must forgive me for not having answered hers. I engage to write her the first one I send forth beyond the size of a note, and I trust she will not expect it the less early or the less kindly for my not promising any particular day for it. I send her as many kisses as she would put up with from a sick face, and those, I know, would be not a few, were it for nothing but sick friendship's sake. Do you hear that, dear Mary? and will you, or Shelley, write me another letter beforehand to tell me how you are? Marianne used to come behind me and put an Italian letter before my eyes, as a charm to take the jaundice out of them. And yet I – Well, no matter. You see what it is to have an impudent fellow for a friend, who reckons on his being pardoned; but I hope to mend all my ungrateful faults with my health. Not a word of review have I written yet upon *Prometheus Unbound*, but I must say for myself that it was out of a consciousness that I should have a go at length into it, and so a fear to begin, that I delayed so long; not forgetting, however, that I did not expect to be able to make so abstract and *odi-profanum* a poem at all recommendable to readers in general; but it ought to have had my homage at all events, and so should the divine Ode on the Skylark: –

κοορὸν καὶ πτηνὸν καὶ ἱερον.[1]

Poor Keats! have you heard of him? They send word from Rome that he is dying; and he is so fearfully sensitive he cannot even bear to receive news from England: but I hope to the last, especially as I have seen remarkable recoveries in consumptive cases. I must leave off. My head began reeling in the middle of the last page. – Your affectionate   Leigh Hunt

To Joseph Severn

Vale of Health, Hampstead,
8 March 1821

Dear Severn, – You have concluded, of course, that I have sent no letters to Rome, because I was aware of the effect they would have on Keats's mind; and this is the principal cause; for, besides what I have been told about letters in Italy, I remember his telling me upon one occasion that, in his sick moments, he never wished to receive another letter, or ever to see another face, however friendly. But still I should have written to you, had I not been almost at death's door myself. You will imagine how ill I have been, when you hear that I have but just begun writing again for the *Examiner* and *Indicator*, after an interval of several months, during which my flesh wasted from me with sickness and melancholy. Judge how often I thought of Keats, and with what feelings. Mr Brown tells me he is comparatively calm now, or rather quite so. If he can bear to hear of us, pray tell him; but he knows it already, and can put it in better language than any man. I hear that he does not like to be told that he may get better; nor is it to be wondered at, considering his firm persuasion that he shall not survive. He can only regard it as a puerile thing, and an insinuation that he shall die. But if his persuasion should happen to be no longer so strong, or if he can now put up with attempts to console him, of what I have said a thousand times, and what I still (upon my honour) think always, that I have seen too many instances of recovery from apparently desperate cases of consumption not to be in hope to the very last. If he still cannot bear this, tell him – tell that great poet and noble-hearted man – that we shall bear his memory in the most precious part of our hearts, and that the world shall bow their heads to it, as our loves do. Or if this, again, will trouble his spirit, tell him that we shall never cease to remember and love him; and that, Christian or infidel, the most sceptical of us has faith enough in the high things that nature puts into our heads, to think all who are of one accord in mind or heart are journeying to one and the same place, and shall unite somewhere or other again, face to face, mutually conscious, mutually delighted. Tell him he is only before us on the road, as he is in everything else; or, whether you tell him the latter or no, tell him the former, and add that we shall never forget that he was so, and that we are coming after him. The tears are again in my eyes, and I must not afford to shed them. The next letter I write shall be more to yourself, and more refreshing to your spirits, which we are very sensible must have been greatly taxed. But whether your friend dies or not, it will not be among the least lofty of your recollections by-and-by that you helped to smooth the sick-bed of so fine a being. God bless you, dear Severn. Your sincere friend,   Leigh Hunt

(Keats in fact had died on 23 February.)

To Percy Bysshe Shelley

Stonehouse, near Plymouth, 26th March, 1822
My dearest Friend, – Your letters always contain something delightful to me, whatever news they bring.

'Surgit *amici* aliquid, quod in ipsis *nubibus ardet.*'[2]

But I confess your latter ones have greatly relieved me on the subject you speak of. They only make me long, with an extreme Homeric longing, to be at Pisa, – I mean such an one as Achilles felt when he longed to be with his father, – sharp in his very limbs. We have secured a ship, the *David Walter*, which will call for us here, and sets sail from London in a fortnight. I have written by to-day's post with intelligence of it to Mrs Fletcher, enclosing her the letter, and giving her the option of going on board in London, or here. I need not say we shall attend to her comforts in every respect. The same post also carries a letter to Mr Gisborne, stating your wishes, and wonders respecting *Adonais*. If it is not published before I leave England, I will publish

170

my criticism upon the Pisa copy, – a criticism which I think you will like. I take the opportunity of showing the public the reason why Gifford's review spoke so bitterly of *Prometheus,* and why it pretends that the most metaphysical passage of your most metaphysical poem is a specimen of the clearness of your general style. The wretched priest-like cunning and undertoned malignity of that review of *Prometheus* is indeed a homage paid to qualities which can so provoke it. The *Quarterly* pretends now, that it never meddles with you personally, – of course it never did! For this, *Blackwood* cries out upon it, contrasting its behaviour in those delicate matters with its own! This is better and better, and the public seem to think so; for these things, depend upon it, are getting better understood every day, and shall be better and better understood every day to come. One circumstance which helps to reconcile me to having been detained on this coast, is the opportunity it has given me to make your works speak for themselves wherever I could; and you are in high lustre I assure you, with the most intelligent circles in Plymouth, ἀστὴρ ἐψος.[3] I have, indeed, been astonished to find how well prepared people of intelligence are to fall in with your aspirations, and despise the mistakes and rascally instincts of your calumniators. This place, for instance, abounds in *schoolmasters,* who appear, to a man, to be liberal to an extreme and esoterical degree. And such, there is reason to believe, is the case over the greater part of the kingdom, greatly, no doubt, owing to political causes. Think of the consequences of this with the rising generation. I delight in *Adonais.* It is the most Delphic poetry I have seen a long while; full of those embodyings of the most subtle and airy imaginations, – those arrestings and explanations of the most shadowy yearnings of our being – which are the most difficult of all things to put into words, and the most delightful when put. I do not know whether you are aware how fond I am of your song on the Skylark; but you ought, if Ollier sent you a copy of the enlarged *Calendar of Nature,* which he published separately under the title of the *Months.* I tell you this, because I have not done half or a twentieth part of what I ought to have done to make your writings properly appreciated. But I intended to do more every day, and now that I am coming to you, I shall be *totus* in you and yours! For all good, and healthy, and industrious things, I will do such wonders, that I shall begin to believe I make some remote approach to something like a return for your kindness. Yet how can that be? At all events, I hope we shall all be the better for one another's society. Marianne, poor dear girl, is still very ailing and weak, but stronger upon the whole, she thinks, than when she first left London, and quite prepared and happy to set off on her spring voyage. She sends you part of her best love. I told her I supposed I must answer Marina's [Mary Shelley] letter for her, but she is quite grand on the occasion, and vows she will do it herself, which, I assure you, will be the first time she has written a line for many months. Ask Marina if she will be charitable, and write one to me. I will undertake to answer it with one double as long. But what am I talking about, when the captain speaks of sailing in a fortnight? I was led astray by her delightful letter to Marianne about walks, and duetts, and violets, and ladies like violets. Am I indeed to see and be in the midst of all these beautiful things, ladies like lilies not excepted? And do the men in Italy really leave ladies to walk in those very amiable dry ditches by themselves? Oh! for a few strides like those of Neptune, when he went from some place to some other place, and 'did it in three!' Dear Shelley, I am glad my letter to Lord B. pleased you, though I do not know why you should so thank me for it. But you are ingenious in inventing claims for me upon your affection. – Your affectionate Leigh Hunt

P.S. – Speaking of duetts (in which I fear Marina will find me a much worse performer by the side of Mrs Williams, than her regard for the little parlour makes her paint to her memory), I bring with me some music, among which are three operas of Mozart, for the piano, and a collection of the only songs of Winter published in this country; among the latter is the duett of Vaglil-lotti, which you said was *too* beautiful and melancholy.

To Horace Smith[1]

Pisa, 25 July 1822

Dear Horace, – I trust that the first news of the dreadful calamity which has befallen us here will have been broken to you by report, otherwise I shall come upon you with a most painful abruptness; but Shelley, my divine-minded friend, your friend, the friend of the universe, he has perished at sea. He was in a boat with his friend Captain Williams, going from Leghorn to Lerici, when a storm arose, and it is supposed the boat must have foundered. It was on the 8th instant, about four or five in the evening, they guess. A fisherman says he saw the boat a few minutes before it went down; he looked again and it was gone. He saw the boy they had with them aloft furling one of the sails. We hope his story is true, as their passage from life to death will then have been short; and what adds to the hope is, that in S.'s pocket (for the bodies were both thrown on shore some days afterwards, – conceive our horrible certainty, after trying all we could to hope!) a copy of Keats's last volume, which he had borrowed of me to read on his passage, was found *open* and doubled back as if it had been thrust in, in the hurry of a surprise. God bless him! I cannot help thinking of him as if he were alive as much as ever, so unearthly he always appeared to me, and so seraphical a thing of the elements; and this is what all his friends say. But, what we all feel, your own heart will tell you.

I am only just stronger enough than Mrs S. at present to write you this letter; but shall do very well. Our first numbers will shortly appear; though this, like everything else, however important to us, looks like an impertinence just now. God bless you. Mrs H. sends her best remembrances to you and Mrs Smith, and so does your obliged and sincere friend,   Leigh Hunt

It has often been feared that Shelley and Captain Williams would meet with some accident, they were so hazardous; but when they set out on the 8th, in the morning it was fine. Our dear friend was passionately fond of the sea, and has been heard to say he

173

should like it to be his death-bed.

I think Mrs S. told me yesterday that she should like to be informed of anything you may happen to know respecting his affairs. I can spare you a morsel of a lock of his hair, if you have none.

From T.B. Macaulay

War Office, 27 March 1841

My dear Sir, – I have just had a long conversation with Lord Melbourne, on whom I have pressed your claims with as much urgency as I thought myself justified in using. I have not time to give you particulars, some of which would be curious and amusing. At last he told me that he feared a pension was out of the question, but that he would try to do something for you. This is less than I wished, but more, I own, than I expected.

I assure you that your letter has affected me much. I am sorry and ashamed for my country, that a man of so much merit should have endured so much distress.

I heard the other day, from one of poor Southey's nephews, that he cannot live many weeks: I really do not see why you might not succeed him. The title of Poet Laureate is indeed ridiculous. But the salary ought to be left for the benefit of some man of letters. Should the present government be in office when a vacancy takes place, I really think that the matter might be managed. – Believe me, my dear sir, yours very faithfully   T.B. Macaulay

From *Leigh Hunt's Journal*

With regard to the Laureateship, the editor of this journal has particular reasons for wishing to give his opinion on the subject in his own person; and his opinion is, that if the office in future is really to be bestowed on the highest degree of poetical merit, and on that only (as, being a solitary office, it unquestionably ought to be, though such has not hitherto been the case), then Mr Alfred Tennyson is entitled to it above any other man in the kingdom; since of all living poets he is the most gifted with the sovereign poetical faculty, Imagination. May he live to wear his laurel to a green old age; singing congratulations to Queen Victoria and human advancement, long after the writer of these words shall have ceased to hear him with mortal ears.

7 December 1850

To Thomas Moore

32 Edwardes Square, Kensington
8 June 1841

The remembrance of other days makes me dislike to call you 'Sir', and for obvious reasons it might not be proper to say 'Dear Sir', yet this letter comes to own to Mr Moore how sorry I was, this morning, to find that he had reprinted the verses from *The Times*.[1] I confess I should almost as soon have expected their republication in your collected works (a packet for posterity), as I should have thought of repeating the letters from the *Tatler* in the selection of papers lately published under the title of the *Seer*. Not that I take upon me to assume that those papers will last beyond my life, but because I had flattered myself that there were good qualities enough on both sides to merit the survival of esteem beyond a day of hostility; and because I have taken repeated opportunities, for years past, of showing that it had long ceased on my side, and of mentioning your name with the cheerful admiration that belongs to it. That of Lord Byron himself, for an equal space of time, has been treated by me with nothing but respect for the respect due to his poetry; and I have often expressed my regrets at my former remarks on him, not because they were not

175

true, – for they were, – critical errors excepted; but because a better knowledge of myself has taught me that no one frail human being has a right to sit in that manner in judgment on another. If, indeed, any imaginary circumstance should have induced you to misconstrue these evidences of good-will, all I can say is, that I have never written a syllable, during these late years, with the intention of wounding you, and that I never utter a syllable in private at variance with that I write. How could I renew hostilities, after consenting (permit me to use that word on the present occasion) to receive a favour from you, – the subscription to my 'Poems'? and allow me to ask, how could you, after I had received the favour, suffer the attack on me to be reprinted? I will not, on many accounts, add the special reasons I have at this moment for wishing that it had not been done. Should you take occasion from this letter, at any future time, to show your accordance with that wish, let me say, that you will only do for me that I have learnt to do for all mankind; namely, to be as considerate to them as I can. Should it appear to you best to take no notice of the wish or the letter, then or now, I shall console myself with reflecting that I neither expect you to answer it if you wish not, nor shall think the better or worse of myself in future, for retaining, unmoved, the charities which adversity has taught me. I have the honour to be Mr Moore's old admirer and very sincere humble servant, Leigh Hunt

To B.W. Procter[1]

Hammersmith, 10 October 1857

My Dear Procter, – I was extremely gratified with the sight of Mr Hawthorne, his *Scarlet Letter* having given me a desire to know a man so full of thought, and feeling, and fine purpose. His few words do not hinder his countenance from being one of the most speaking I ever met with; and I flatter myself he will say more to me when I see him again.

The letter he brought me, too, gave great pleasure to your old and never-forgetting friend. I wish you would give me a *tête-à-tête* some evening before long in Weymouth Street, and then I will give you good reasons why you must indulge me with one in my loneliness at Hammersmith. – Ever truly yours,   Leigh Hunt

To B.W. Procter

23 June 1857

...That York should appear to you 'the most desolate city in England', surprised me. One fancies those famous cities to remain always what they were. I suppose the railways run away with the inhabitants to London and elsewhere. When I say 'what they were', I mean in point of substance and occupancy: otherwise no old city in the times in which we live, unless it be absolutely deserted (as I have seen a town on the coast of Italy), or grass-grown in some of its streets, like Verona, can affect us with a sense of former ages, as it does in books. What are all the houses in York to the houses of 'York and Lancaster'? and did you ever think of York at all, old or new, when the 'Duke of York' was commander-in-chief? How different he sounded from the Duke Richards and Edwards! I got a strong ancient sensation once out of Chester, with its walls, and its curious-lifted corridors and footways; yet, inasmuch as the waiters said, 'Yes, sir,' and there was 'Smith, grocer,' over shop-doors, the living impression would not let the old one alone; no, not though I saw the river Dee, on which King Edgar was rowed by eight kinglets, and for two or three minutes the 'wizard stream' looked verily enchanted, the day was so hot, and everything was so still and motionless. Death, however, making dreadful distances between past and present, I do not wonder that you felt as you did at suddenly meeting with Etty[2] in the shape of a tomb-stone, but why should you end with calling what you say about it 'gossiping nonsense'? I have observed more than once in you of late a tendency to

177

undervalue what you say, and to call it 'words,' as if words were not often things also, and very precious, especially on the gravest occasions. I am afraid your very generosity has helped to mislead you in the matter, as well as your acquaintance with less generous men. But it becomes all who are sincere to stick by one another, whether able or not to prove their sincerity, at all times, to the incredulous. So, as a party greatly interested in the value of words (since I possess little else), I must beg you to turn aside from those gentlemen, and from your own experience of the law, and never to speak otherwise than becomes the man you are and a poet; for without 'words,' and the truth of things that is in them, what were we!

A pretty lecture! yet I think I am older enough, as well as poorer enough, to be allowed to give it. Adversity and bad health conspired to isolate me for so many years, not having a crust, as it were, with which even to greet a friend, or a penny for coach-hire wherewith to seek him, that I began to be base enough to think my own best words of consequence to nobody even when about themselves. Great was my joy at finding the case otherwise; and this is another reason why I must not have words undervalued by those whom I have never ceased to think sincere, however their own depreciation of their words may have pretended to puzzle me. I have also another reason, which I particularly desire to whisper in your ear whenever I can speak apart with you *viva voce* for five minutes, and which it was of no use to tell before. And it is a very delightful reason too, at least to myself, and you will like it on that account. So come for the riddle as soon as you can.

I wish I could make it worth ——'s while to come and talk French with *me*, for though I can 'read French' (as the advertisements say), I 'cannot speak it'. I would get on very quickly too, septuagenarian though I be; and then I should not be ashamed, as I was the other day, when Monckton Milnes introduced me to Mons. Merimée, ' who spoke English'. Yet I was glad of it too; and I bask in the brusque geniality of the said Monckton, who is a good fellow and large-brained withal. Item, his wife hath a smile as sweet as a sudden piece of good news. . . .

Going from 'madhouse to madhouse' is indeed earning good payment hardly, especially for a poet; but then he is the man to do all the good possible to people so terribly out of the pale of commonplace, for he is used to those regions of imagination to which non-use or want of the complete round of brain has subjected them; and I have no doubt your pilgrimages have carried blessings with them. This must be, and of course is, your consolation. This year, I suspect, has been a particularly trying year to all delicate organization, and you will probably find yourself younger again next. Meantime 'St. Leon' or 'the milk' won't do, will they? unless people could recover those whom they have lost, and by whom, during the fatigue of advanced life, they often feel willing to lie down 'under the green turf,' till the thought of survivors sets them again in motion. In one respect, besides the greater regard which I retain for 'words,' my sequestered unlegal, *i.e.* unlaw-mingled life (a terrible compound epithet that, I must own) has given me an advantage over you in keeping alive my tendency to see loveabilities in people, and thus to add to my stock of comforts; for I do not the less love old friends — quite the contrary – for when good-heartedness survives all trials and exacerbations, where can loveability be so well proved? Besides, I have grandchildren, which is a help in this matter to which you have not attained; and two of them live in the house with me, and think I take as much interest in what they do as if I were no older; which is a wonderful flattery to the would-be inconvenience in the 'old Adam,' and tends to make him fancy that he has as much right to remain in the borders of their paradise as they have to be in it, if for no better reason than his wish to do so, and his sorrows.

But I am answering every point in your letter, with a vengeance! and have been cramming the previous page with small writing, out of a fear, that overtook me in the leaf before it, of my having no more room! whereas I am going to leave a couple of blank pages! However, it will show you, my dear old friend, how glad I am to have a talk with you, and how it bears me on, in spite of all languid, and hot, and cephalic, and dyspeptic misgivings of

179

ability. So come to see me as soon as you can, as be assured I will you; only, mind, that it must be under circumstances during which I can speak to you for a few minutes apart. It is nothing that can put you out in any way; only something which I must call to your mind. But I think I can take you better apart (if you do not come alone), from several persons than from one: so your family first, if you please, and Forster afterwards. Or I will first come to Weymouth Street if you prefer it, and then Forster can be met, and all, after which I shall propose to join you some evening in Montagu Square.

See, one of my two remaining pages is gone, after all; and I am writing haphazard by twilight. Twilight! past *nine*. Ever truly yours (I would say 'affectionately' if you didn't somehow dash my young septuagenarian blood, notwithstanding your verses), Leigh Hunt

(A good enough signature that. Dinner and tea brought back strength to my fingers, June 24.)

To Mr and Mrs Browning[1]

Hammersmith, 17 November, 1857

My dear Friends, – Though I was extremely glad at the sight of your kind letter, and have ever since been wondering how I could refrain from telling you on the instant, yet being occupied with pressing correspondence at the time, I became delayed, partly by the languor which always ensues with me on exertion, but chiefly by an old and in vain constantly punished habit which I have, of thinking I must needs write replies to letters which interest me very much, as long and as full of matter as the satisfaction which they give me. I am very sorry, particularly on an occasion like this; for when friends express regret for anything, I always feel as if such subjection to myself put me in the wrong with them, and as if I had nothing to do but to go down lower on my own knees, and express my greater regret for having subjected them to the subjection. At all events, you will see, that the delay of weeks on such an occasion becomes, in my mind, something quite as much needing pardon, as that of months on the other; for if the idea of what it was incumbent on me to do in return for a letter of reasonable dimensions became the vast thing which I speak of, what must have been the case with yourselves, when the mere sight of such a huge epistle as mine must have visited you with a sense of a monster of responsibility at once? I do not, I assure you (as after these confessions you may easily believe, and I could give you more, if you needed them), at all wonder at your putting off the day of answering, especially considering the successions of circumstances you speak of, including the illness of your boy, the terribleness of whose beauty at such a time I can well imagine; for though I have not seen it myself in such beauty physical, I have, several times, in beauty spiritual and leave-taking, still more terrible to remember, for the leave-taking was well founded; I dare not say more yet, except that I now feel to belong almost as much to the next world as to this. The common places of this world often appear very strange to me, and the uncommon places of the next, as if they must needs be things household and familiar, and the only explainers, and reconcilers to themselves, of that other, imperfected wonder: as indeed, thank God, I believe they will be.

I forgot to say, dear Mrs Browning, at the beginning of my letter, that one of the accumulators of the causes of my delay was a theological temptation occasioned me by a passage in your letter which you will readily call to mind, but which I found it would be impossible for me to discuss, I should again have become so voluminous, and, I little doubt, so unsatisfactory. This you will readily believe when I tell you that the only two books of paramount authority with me are the Book of Nature, and the heart of its reader, Man; and that the operations in the one, and the aspirations of the other (though I fully concede, as I am bound to do, all the reconcilements, and possibilities, and transcendentations of every kind, which greater understandings and imaginations than my own may see in other books), compel me – if so glad a conclusion can be called compulsion – to be of the opinion that God is the unmingled, wholly benevolent, and conscious Spirit of Good, working through His agent, Man; that evil, where it *is* evil, and not a necessary portion of good (as it probably all is ultimately), is the difficulty presented to the course of this working by the unconscious, involuntary, and therefore unmalignant, mystery called Matter; that God, though not immediately or in all stages of His processes almighty, is ultimately so; and that His constant occupation is the working out of heavens in place and time, in which prospection and retrospection somehow or other become reconciled to the final conscious beatitude of all the souls that have ever existed: – See! I have not been able to avoid my theology at last! – as to not letting you sit by me, most pleased and honoured shall I feel myself if you will let me sit on any form of good-natured allowance by *you*. Your husband, I think, would be equally charitable. I have not addressed you two separately in this letter, except as I might by turns, if sitting with you in a room; though I feel that you have separately addressed myself for very kind reasons on this special occasion. I have also left myself little more room in this sheet of paper, and I dare not take another for fear of again running out of bounds and making my head giddy. But not the less, dear Robert Browning, do I thank you for all which you have said to me so warm-heartedly about yourself, about myself, about the divine Portuguese sonnets, about Kenyon,[2] about Shelley, about everything, of the gracious words to me of your wife. God bless you both, and enable me to live to commune with you again in person before I rejoin the dear ones with whom I trust we shall be some day in company together. – Your obliged and affectionate   Leigh Hunt

William Hazlitt

We shall conclude with a short notice of an individual who, in the cast of his mind and in political principle, bears no very remote resemblance to the patriot and wit just spoken of [Thomas Moore], and on whose merits we should descant at greater length, but that personal intimacy might be supposed to render us partial. It is well when personal intimacy produces this effect; and when the light, that dazzled us at a distance, does not on a closer inspection turn out an opaque substance.

This is a charge that none of his friends will bring against Mr Leigh Hunt. He improves upon acquaintance. The author translates admirably into the man. Indeed, the very faults of his style are virtues in the individual. His natural gaiety and sprightliness of manner, his high animal spirits, and the *vinous* quality of his mind, produce an immediate fascination and intoxication in those who come in contact with him, and carry of insociety whatever in his writings may to some seem flat and impertinent. From great sanguiness of temper, from great quickness and unsuspecting simplicity, he runs on to the public as he does at his own fire-side, and talks about himself, forgetting that he is not always among friends. His look, his tone are required to point many things that he says: his frank, cordial manner reconciles you instantly to a little over-bearing, over-weening self-complacency. 'To be admired, he needs but to be seen': but perhaps he ought to be seen to be fully appreciated. No one ever sought his society who did not come away with a more favourable opinion of him: no one was ever disappointed, except those who had entertained idle prejudices against him. He sometimes trifles with his readers, or tires of a subject (from not being urged on by the stimulus of immediate sympathy); but in conversation he is all life and animation, combining the vivacity of the school-boy with the resources of the wit and the taste of the scholar. The personal character, the spontaneous impulses, do not appear to excuse the author, unless you are acquainted with his situation and habits: like some great beauty who gives herself what we think strange airs and graces under a mask, but who is instantly forgiven when she shews her face.

The Spirit of the Age
1825

Thomas Carlyle

...Hunt is always ready to go and walk with me, or sit and talk with me, to all lengths, if I want him: he comes in some once a week (when invited, for he is very modest), takes a cup of tea, and sits discoursing, in his brisk fanciful way, till supper-time, and then cheerfully *eats* a cup of porridge (to sugar only), which he praises to the skies, and vows he will make his supper of at home. He is a man of thoroughly London make, such as you could not find elsewhere, and I think about the *best* possible to be made of his sort. An airy, crotchetty, most copious, clever Talker, with an honest undercurrent of *reason* too, but unfortunately not the deepest, not the most practical; or rather is the most *un*practical ever man dealt in. His hair is grizzled, eyes black-hazel, complexion of the clearest dusky-brown; a thin glimmer of smile plays over a face of cast-iron gravity; giving him a singular, discrepant air. He never *laughs*, can only *titter*; which I think indicates his worst deficiency. In figure and complexion he somewhat reminds me of our late Uncle Sandy: there is the same honest cheerful look, tho' so differently expressed. I reckon Hunt a thoroughly sincere man; and find him entertaining by a time. His House here excels all you have ever read of; a 'poetical Tinkerdom' without parallel even in Literature. In his family-room, where are a sickly large Wife and a whole shoal of well-conditioned wild children, you will find half a dozen old rickety chairs gathered from half a dozen different hucksters, and all seemingly engaged, and just pausing, in a violent *hornpipe*; on these, and around them, and over the dusty table and ragged carpet, lie all kinds of litter; books, papers, egg-shells, pil[lows?] and, last night when I was there, the *torn heart* of a half quartern loaf! His own room above stairs, into which alone I strive to enter, he keeps cleaner; it has only two chairs, a book-case and a writing-table: yet the noble Hunt receives you in his Tinkerdom with the spirit of a King; apologizes for nothing; places you in the best seat; takes a window-sill himself, if there is no other, and then folding closer his loose-flowing 'muslin-cloud' of a printed night-gown (in which he always writes), commences the liveliest dialogue on Philosophy and the Prospects of Man (who is to be beyond measure 'happy' yet), which again he will courteously terminate the moment you are bound to go. A most interesting, pitiable, loveable man; to be used kindly, but with discretion.

Letter to Alexander Carlyle
27 June 1834

Our commonest evening sitter, for a good while, was Leigh Hunt, who lived close by, and delighted to sit talking with us (free, cheery, idly melodious as bird on bough) or listening, with real feeling to her [Mrs Carlyle's] old Scotch tunes on the piano, and winding up with a frugal morsel of Scotch porridge (endlessly admirable to Hunt)...Hunt was always accurately dressed these evenings, and had a fine chivalrous gentlemanly carriage, polite, affectionate, respectful (especially to her) and yet so free and natural...His household, while at 4 Upper Cheyne Row, within a few steps of us here, almost at once disclosed itself to be hugger-mugger, unthrift and sordid collapse, once for all; and had to be associated with on cautious terms, while he himself emerged out of it in the chivalrous figure I describe. Dark complexion (a trace of the African, I believe), copious clean strong black hair, beautifully-shaped head, fine beaming serious hazel eyes; serious and intellect the main expression of the face (to our surprise at first), – he would lean on his elbow against the mantelpiece (fine clean, elastic figure too he had, five feet ten or more), and look round him nearly in silence, before taking leave for the night, 'as if I were a Lar,' said he once, 'or permanent Household God here!' (such his polite, Ariel-like way). Another time, rising from this Lar attitude, he repeated (voice very fine) as if in sport of parody, yet with something of very sad perceptible: 'While I to sulphurous and penal fire' – as the last thing before vanishing.

Carlyle, *Reminiscences*,
ed. Charles Eliot Norton, 1887, vol. I

Nathaniel Hawthorne

Leigh Hunt was then (1855) at Hammersmith occupying a very plain and shabby little house, in a contiguous range of others like it, with no prospect but that of an ugly village street, and certainly nothing to gratify his craving for a tasteful environment inside or out. A slatternly maid-servant opened the door for us, and he himself stood in the entry, a beautiful and venerable old man, buttoned to the chin in an old black dresscoat, tall and slender, with a countenance quietly alive all over, and the gentlest and most naturally courteous manner. He ushered us into his little study, or parlour, or both – a very forlorn room, with poor paper-hangings, and carpet, few books, no pictures that I remember, and an awful lack of upholstery. I touch distinctly upon these external blemishes and this nudity of adornment, not that they would be worth mentioning in a sketch of other remarkable persons, but because Leigh Hunt was born with such a faculty for enjoying all beautiful things that it seemed as if Fortune did him as much wrong in not supplying them, as in withholding a sufficiency of vital breath from ordinary men.

Our Old Home
1863

Charles Dickens

Harold Skimpole is introduced:

He was a little bright creature, with a large head; but a delicate face, and a sweet voice, and there was a perfect charm in him. All he said was so free from effort and spontaneous, and was said with such a captivating gaiety that it was fascinating to hear him talk... There was an easy negligence in his manner, and even in his dress (his hair carelessly disposed, and his neckerchief loose and flowing, as I have seen artists paint their own portrait) which I could not separate from the idea of a romantic youth who had undergone some unique process of depreciation....

He must confess to two of the oldest infirmities in the world: one was, that he had no idea of time; the other, that he had no idea of money. In consequence of which, he never kept an appointment, never could transact any business, and never knew the value of anything!   (Chapter VI)

Harold Skimpole at home:

(His room] was dingy enough, and not at all clean; but furnished with an odd kind of shabby luxury, with a large footstool, a sofa, and plenty of cushions, an easy-chair, and plenty of pillows, a piano, books, drawing materials, music, newspapers, and a few sketches and pictures. A broken pane of glass in one of the dirty windows was papered and wafered over; but there was a little plate of hothouse nectarines on the table, and there was another of grapes, and another of sponge-cake, and there was a bottle of light wine. Mr Skimpole himself reclined upon the sofa, in a dressing-gown, drinking some fragrant coffee from an old china cup – it was then about midday – and looking at a collection of wall-flowers on the balcony.   (Chapter XLIII)

Harold Skimpole speaks for himself:

... speaking of himself as if he were not at all his own affair, as if Skimpole were a third person, as if he knew that Skimpole had his singularities, but still had claims too, which were the general business of the community and must not to be slighted....

'I covet nothing...Possession is nothing to me. Here is my friend Jarndyce's excellent house. I feel obliged to him for possessing it. I can sketch it, and alter it. I can set it to music. When I am here, I have sufficient possession of it, and have neither trouble, cost, nor responsibility...having Harold Skimpole, a confiding child, petitioning you, the world, an agglomeration of practical people of business habits, to let him live and admire the human family, do it somehow or other, like good souls, and suffer him to ride his rocking-horse!...It's only you, the generous creatures, whom I envy...I envy you your power of doing what you do. It is what I should revel in myself. I don't feel any vulgar gratitude to you. I almost feel as if *you* ought to be grateful to *me*, for giving you the opportunity of enjoying the luxury of generosity. I know you like it. For anything I can tell, I may have come into the world expressly for the purpose of increasing your stock of happiness. I may have been born to be a benefactor to you, by sometimes giving you an opportunity of assisting me in my little perplexities. Why should I regret my incapacity for details and worldly affairs, when it leads to such pleasant consequences? I don't regret it therefore.'   (Chapter VI)

Bleak House
1853

John Forster

Harold Skimpole, recognisable for Leigh Hunt, led to much remark; the difference being, that ludicrous traits were employed in the first to enrich without impairing an attractive person in the tale, whereas to the last was assigned a part in the plot which no fascinating foibles or gaieties of speech could redeem from contempt. Though a want of consideration was thus shown to the friend whom the character would be likely to recall to many readers, it is nevertheless very certain that the intention of Dickens was not at first, or at any time, an unkind one. He erred from thoughtlessness only. What led him to the subject at all, he has himself stated. Hunt's philosophy of moneyed obligations, always, though loudly, half jocosely proclaimed, and his ostentatious wilfulness in the humouring of that or any other theme on which he cared for the time to expatiate, had so often seemed to Dickens to be whimsical and attractive that, wanting an 'airy quality' for the man to be invented, this of Hunt occurred to him . . .

The Life of Charles Dickens
1872-4, vol. II, chap. VII

Charles Dickens to Leigh Hunt

As it gives you so much pain, I take it at its worst, and say I am deeply sorry, and that I feel I did wrong in doing it, but I maintain that there is nothing it that should have given you pain . . . When I felt it was going too close I stopped myself, and the most blotted parts of my MS are those in which I have been striving hard to make the impression I was writing from UNlike you. The character is not you, for there are traits in it common to fifty thousand people besides, and I did not fancy you would ever recognize it.

28 June 1855

Notes

The Story of Rimini
1 In a note to the 1855 edition, Hunt informs his readers: 'The greater portion of this poem was written in the prison to which the author, then editor of *The Examiner*, was condemned for some severe remarks on the Prince Regent, at a time when freedom of speech was not allowed to the press as abundantly and wisely as it is now; and the state of his health was such as to render confinement more than ordinarily injurious.'

2 Canto IV of the poem recounts how, afflicted with melancholy and guilt, Paulo and Francesca discontinue their clandestine meetings. Unwittingly, Francesca reveals the affair to Giovanni when she cries out in her sleep. Challenged to a duel by his revenging brother, Paulo allows himself to fall on Giovanni's sword. When Francesca is brought to the room where the body has been laid, she dies in an attitude of prayerful grief. Unlike Dante, Hunt leaves uncertain the consummation of the love, but the sympathy he evoked for the lovers in this version was received controversially by his readers.

The alteration Hunt made for the 1844 edition involved omitting the first 427 lines, substituting a passage less than quarter of the length. He places the lovers in their bower, where Giovanni, informed by a spy, apprehends and slays them. He retained the original concluding lines, in which the bodies are returned to Ravenna for burial in a single grave.

Captain Sword and Captain Pen
1 Leigh Hunt's Postscript to the 1835 edition of the poem:
The object of this poem is to show the horrors of war, the false ideas of power produced in the minds of its leaders, and, by inference, the unfitness of those leaders for the government of the world. . . .

Even if nothing else were to come of inquiries into the horrors of war, surely they would cry aloud for some better provision against their extremity *after* battle – for some regulated and certain assistance to the wounded and agonized – so that we might hear no longer of men left in cold and misery all night, writhing with torture – of bodies stripped by prowlers, perhaps murderers – and of frenzied men, the other day the darling of their friends, dying, two and even several days after the battle,

190

of famine! The field of Waterloo was not completely cleared of its dead and dying till nearly a week! Surely large companies of men should be organized for the sole purpose of assisting and clearing away the field after battle. They should be steady men, not lightly admitted, nor unpossessed of some knowledge of surgery, and they should be attached to the surgeon's staff. Both sides would respect them for their office, and keep them sacred from violence. . . .

I firmly believe, that war, or the sending of thousands of our fellow creatures to cut one another to bits, often for what they have no concern in, nor understand, will one day be reckoned far more absurd than if people were to settle an argument over the dinner-table with their knives – a logic indeed, which was once fashionable in some places during the 'good old times'. The world has seen the absurdity of that practice; why should it not come to years of discretion, with respect to violence on a larger scale? The other day, our own country and the United States agreed to refer a point of dispute to the arbitration of the king of Holland; a compliment (if we are to believe the newspapers) of which his majesty was justly proud. He struck a medal on the strength of it, which history will show as a set-off against his less creditable attempts to force his opinions upon the Belgians. Why should not every national dispute be referred, in like manner, to a third party? There is reason to suppose that the judgement would stand a good chance of being impartial; and it would benefit the character of the judge, and dispose him to receive judgements of the same kind; till at length the custom would prevail, like any other custom; and men be astonished at the customs that preceded it. In private life, none but schoolboys and the vulgar settle disputes by blows; even duelling is losing its dignity.

William Hazlitt on the poem:
'We should recommend everybody, just now that the war spirit is rising amongst us, to read the poem, and learn what horrors they are rejoicing over, and what the Christian spirit of this age demands of us.'

Rondeau
1   We shall conclude this article with an observation or two, occasioned by a *rondeau* in the volume (Pope's *Letters*), not otherwise very mentionable.

The first is, that in its time, and till lately, it was almost the only rondeau, we believe, existing in the language, certainly the only one that had attracted notice; secondly, that it does not obey the laws of construction laid down by the example of Marot, and pleasantly set forth of late in a publication on '*Rondeaulx*' (pray pronounce the word in good honest old French, with the *eaulx*, like the beating up of eggs for a pudding); third, that owing to the lesser animal spirits prevailing in this country, the larger form of the rondeau is not soon likely to obtain; fourth, that in a smaller and more off-hand shape it seems to us deserving of revival, and extremely well calculated to give effect to such an impulse as naturally inclines us to the repetition of two or three words; and fifth and last, that as love sometimes make people imprudent, and gets them excused for it, so this loving perusal of Pope and his volume has tempted us to publish a rondeau of our own, which was written on a real occasion, and therefore may be presumed to have had the aforesaid impulse. We must add, lest our egotism should be thought still greater on the occasion than it is, that the lady [Jane Carlyle] was a great lover of books and impulsive writers: and that it was our sincerity as one of them which obtained for us the delightful compliment from a young enthusiast to an old one.

> *Men, Women and Books:*
> *Pope, in some lights in which he is not usually regarded*

On the Death of His Son Vincent

1 A year before the death of his son, Hunt published in *Leigh Hunt's Journal* a sonnet by Vincent, 'The Deformed Child'. The first eight lines read:

> An angel prisoned in an infant frame
>   Of mortal sickness and deformity,
> Looks patiently from out that languid eye
> Matured, and seeming large with pain. The name
> Of 'happy childhood' mocks his movements tame,
> Rather than sit, in his frail chair, and try
> To taste the pleasure of that unshared game.

What is Poetry?
1 *Orlando Innamorato* (1487), a poem by Boiardo, recounting Orlando's love for Angelica, princess of Cathay.

Preface to *Stories in Verse*
1 Chaucer, *The Squire's Tale*, lines 1-3.

2 Hunt is referring here to the Crimean War.

3 Chaucer, *The Clerk's Tale*, lines 862-72.

4 The reference is to Job 1.21: 'And said, Naked came I out of my mother's womb, and naked shall I return thither...'

5 *Hudibras*, a satirical poem by Samuel Butler (1612-80).

6 Dryden, *Absalom and Achitophel*, Part I, lines 92-103.

7 Chaucer, *The Knight's Tale*, line 1416.

8 Chaucer, *The Squire's Tale*, line 268.

9 Ibid., lines 76-87.

10 Matthew Prior (1664-1721), a prolific and lively writer, whose early eighteenth century narratives end in coarse jokes; Matthew Green (1697-1737), remembered for his poem, *The Spleen* (1737).

S.T. Coleridge
1 Thomas Shadwell, critic and poet (?1642-92), satirized by Dryden in his poems *MacFlecknoe* and *The Medal*.

2 Revd Edward Irving (1792-1834), a popular Presbyterian minister.

3 The family of James Gillman, with whom Coleridge lived from 1818 until his death in 1834.

Lord Byron
1 Thomas Moore (1779-1852), the 'national bard' of Ireland, through his *Irish Melodies* (1801-34), and close friend of Byron, whose life he wrote.

2   William Bowles (1762-1850), author of *Fourteen Sonnets* (1789), and described by Byron as 'the maudlin prince of mournful sonneteers'.

3   The correspondence is not included in this book.

Mr Keats
1   Hunt is referring to an earlier discussion of 'Ode to a Nightingale': 'O for a beaker full of the warm South, / Full of the true, the blushful Hippocrene...'
Hunt's influence on Keats's reputation and his early poetry, for good and ill, is discussed fully by J.R. McGillivray in the introduction to his *Keats: a Bibliography and Reference Guide* (1949), and by Walter Jackson Bate in his biography, *John Keats* (1963), pp.77-82, 184-7.

2   Keats in fact died on 23 February 1821.

Adonais
1   'The poet of Ireland' is Thomas Moore.

2   Shelley describes himself, 'one frail form', in stanza 31 of the poem.

3   'If some untimely blow snatches you, half of my own life, away...' – Horace, *Odes*, II.xvii.5.

4   William Gifford (1756-1826), first editor of the *Quarterly Review*, which published Croker's devastating review of *Endymion*.

5   Mrs Alicia Le Fanu (1753-1817), eldest daughter of Thomas Sheridan, who wrote a 'patriotic comedy', *Sons of Erin or Modern Sentiment*, which was given one performance at the Lyceum Theatre on 13 April 1812. Eaton Stannard Barrett (1786-1820), wrote a eulogy on the virtues and graces of women, *Woman and other poems*, which was published in 1810 and ran to five editions. Mr Howard Payne (1791-1852), American actor and playwright, author of the song 'Home, Sweet Home'.

6   Henry Milman (1791-1868), playwright and Professor of Poetry at Oxford (1821-31).

Review of Tennyson's *Poems*

1   Anna Seward (1747-1809), poet, known as the 'Swan of Lichfield'.

2   Hunt is alluding to *The Merry Wives of Windsor*, conflating two remarks by Sir Hugh: 'Why, it is affectations' (I.i.147), and 'But can you affection me, 'oman?' (I.i.220).

3   'Adeline', stanza V.

4   Robert Merry (1775-98), a poet ridiculed by William Gifford as one of the Della Cruscan group of poets, named after a Florentine academy set up to sift and purify the Italian language.

5   The line is from *The Dunciad*, IV, 252.

6   The quotation is from Ovid, *Metamorphoses* III.466: 'Quod cupio, mecum est; inopem me copia fecit' (Narcissus); 'What I desire, I have. My very plenty makes me poor'.

Distressed Seamen

1   John Wilson Croker (1780-1857), First Lord of the Admiralty and notorious for his criticism of Keats's *Endymion* in the Quarterly Review.

2   Sir Matthew Wood (1768-1843), Lord Mayor of London 1815-17.

3   Thomas Cochrane, later Earl Dundonald (1775-1860), attacked the abuses of the Admiralty. The 'Droits of Admiralty' were rights and perquisites, e.g. proceeds arising from the seizure of enemies' ships, wrecks, etc.

A 'Now' (Hot Day)

1   Dryden says that grasshoppers 'fry' in his 'translation of *Virgil's Gnat* by Spenser, l.163.

2   An allusion to a kind of linen made on the island of Cos, in the Aegean.

A 'Now' (Cold Day)

1   George Cruikshank (1792-1878), caricaturist.

To Marianne Kent
1   Marianne Kent became Hunt's wife in 1809. Their son Thornton described the marriage in an unpublished work, *Proserpina*: 'Fate joined him with one who shared his taste for plastic art, with a greater natural aptitude, but without culture or power of acquiring it; with a childlike sense of verse, never matured; with an almost equally childlike sense of economy which the bookworm long believed to be perfect... with thoughts and sensations so diverse, they were actuated by motives so different, that lengthening years only made them, in the longer portion of their faithful and unsevered union, strangers.'

Autobiography
1   Hunt served his imprisonment at the Horsemonger Lane Prison, Newington Causeway, from February 1813 to February 1815.

2   Thomas Alsager (1779-1873) was the financial editor and music critic of *The Times*.

3   Charles Cowden Clarke (1787-1877), son of Keats's schoolmaster and a close friend of the poet. His reminscences of Keats, Hunt and others may be found in *Recollections of Writers* (1878).

4   In February 1813, Shelley offered £20 to launch a public subscription for payment of Hunt's fine.

To John Keats
1   Keats was staying at Mrs Brawne's, Wentworth Place, his companion George Brown being away in Scotland.

2   Keats had written to Hunt: 'I hope to see you whenever you can get time for I feel really attach'd to you for your many sympathies with me, and patience at my lunes.'

To P.B. Shelley
1   'light and winged and holy', from Plato's *Ion*, where he compares poets to bees.

2 'There rises something of a friend, which blazes amidst the very clouds.'

3 'the morning/eastern star'

To Horace Smith

1 Horatio (Horace) Smith (1779-1849), best known as joint author with his brother of *Rejected Addresses* (1821), parodies of contemporary poetry.

Thomas Moore

1 Moore, under the pseudonym 'T. Pidcock', had published in *The Times* (10 January 1828) his satirical verses 'The Living Dog and the Dead Lion', a thinly veiled attack on Hunt's portrait of Byron in *Lord Byron and his Contemporaries*. A sample verse runs:

However, the book's a good book, being rich in
Examples and warnings to Lions high-bred,
How they suffer small mongrelly curs in their kitchen,
Who'll feed on them living, and foul them when dead.

To B.W. Procter

1 Brian Waller Procter (1787-1874) wrote very popular songs and lyrics under the pseudonym 'Barry Cornwall'. He practised as a solicitor and barrister in London, and was made a commissioner in lunacy – thus the references to 'madhouses' in the next letter.

2 William Etty (1787-1849), considered by many to be the greatest English figure painter, born in York.

To the Brownings

1 Thornton Hunt notes that this letter was found among Hunt's manuscripts, and so was probably a draft.

2 John Kenyon, in whose house *Aurora Leigh* was written and to whom it was dedicated, left the Brownings a large legacy on his death in December 1856.

Fyfield*Books*

Two millennia of essential classics

The extensive Fyfield*Books* list includes

John Lyly *Selected Prose and Dramatic Work*
edited by Leah Scragg

Ben Jonson *Epigrams and The Forest*
edited by Richard Dutton

Giacomo Leopardi *The Canti*
with a selection of his prose
translated by J.G. Nichols

Stéphane Mallarmé *For Anatole's Tomb*
in French and English
translated by Patrick McGuinness

Andrew Marvell *Selected Poems*
edited by Bill Hutchings

Charlotte Mew *Collected Poems and Selected Prose*
edited by Val Warner

Michelangelo *Sonnets*
translated by Elizabeth Jennings,
introduction by Michael Ayrton

William Morris *Selected Poems*
edited by Peter Faulkner

John Henry Newman *Selected Writings to 1845*
edited by Albert Radcliffe

Ovid *Amores*
translated by Tom Bishop

Fernando Pessoa *A Centenary Pessoa*
edited by Eugenio Lisboa and L.C.
Taylor, introduction by Octavio Paz

Petrarch *Canzoniere*
translated by J.G. Nichols

Edgar Allan Poe *Poems and Essays on Poetry*
edited by C.H. Sisson

Restoration Bawdy
edited by John Adlard

Rainer Maria Rilke *Sonnets to Orpheus and Letters to a Young Poet*
translated by Stephen Cohn

Christina Rossetti *Selected Poems*
edited by C.H. Sisson

Dante Gabriel Rossetti *Selected Poems and Translations*
edited by Clive Wilmer

Sir Walter Scott *Selected Poems*
edited by James Reed

Sir Philip Sidney *Selected Writings*
edited by Richard Dutton

John Skelton *Selected Poems*
edited by Gerald Hammond

Charlotte Smith *Selected Poems*
edited by Judith Willson

Henry Howard, Earl of Surrey *Selected Poems*
edited by Dennis Keene

Algernon Charles Swinburne *Selected Poems*
edited by L.M. Findlay

Arthur Symons *Selected Writings*
edited by Roger Holdsworth

William Tyndale *Selected Writings*
edited by David Daniell

Oscar Wilde *Selected Poems*
edited by Malcolm Hicks

William Wordsworth *The Earliest Poems* edited by Duncan Wu

Sir Thomas Wyatt *Selected Poems*
edited by Hardiman Scott

For more information, including a full list of Fyfield*Books* and a contents list for each title, and details of how to order the books in the UK, visit the Fyfield website at www.fyfieldbooks.co.uk or email info@fyfieldbooks.co.uk. For information about Fyfield*Books* available in the United States and Canada, visit the Routledge website at www.routledge-ny.com.